'The principal speakers here were men most eminent in their day; the transactions in which they bore a part have now become history; and some, who were then unborn, may not be unwilling to pass an hour or two in their company, to hear them talk as they did, when they were most at their ease – in a morning-walk or in an evening by the fire-side – and to share what so few, even of their contemporaries, had the privilege of enjoying.' – Samuel Rogers

ROGERS, SAMUEL (1763-1855), author of *Human Life*, man of letters: '"Perhaps you won't go down to posterity at all", said Mr. Dyce, good-naturedly.' [Charles Mackay]. [See *Index of Names*]

Christopher Ricks is Warren Professor of the Humanities and Co-Director of the Editorial Institute at Boston University. He was formerly Professor of Poetry at Oxford.

Samuel Rogers

—

TABLE-TALK & RECOLLECTIONS

—

Selected by
Christopher Ricks

nh Notting Hill Editions

Published in 2011
by Notting Hill Editions Ltd
Newcombe House, 45 Notting Hill Gate
London W11 3LQ

Designed by Flok, Berlin, Germany
Typeset by CB editions, London

Printed and bound
by Memminger MedienCentrum, Memmingen, Germany

Introduction and selection © 2011 by Christopher Ricks

A CIP record for this book
is available from the British Library
ISBN 978-1-907-90336-6

www.nottinghilleditions.com

Contents

Christopher Ricks

– Introduction –

S amuel Rogers was born in Stoke Newington,
30 July 1763, and died in St. James's Place, 18
December 1855. A prolific versifier who indulged not
only *The Pleasures of Memory* (1792) but more largely
those of *Human Life* (1819) as well as of *Italy* (1822,
1828), he was not so lamentable a poet as never even
to be offered the Laureateship. Wordsworth, having
scarcely penned a Laureate line, had died at eighty in
April 1850. Rogers, nearing ninety, sagely passed the
torch to the young Alfred Tennyson (forty-one), who
succeeded in igniting the Laureateship more illumi-
natingly than anyone else has ever done. Tennyson
borrowed, as Wordsworth likewise had once done
for a royal occasion, Rogers's court-suit.

It was not to being a poet that Rogers was
especially suited; rather, a recorder of things said by
wise, witty contemporaries of his. In some ways, as
a diarist who found himself in fortunate company,
he is the William Allingham of the opening half of
the nineteenth century, excepting only (first) that

Allingham had true gifts as a minor poet, creatively intelligent about his talents, and (second) that Allingham was one of the nicest of people. Rogers was distinctly otherwise. Sir Walter Scott remarked, with the needed equanimity, that "It matters not what ill we say of Rogers behind his back, since we may be pretty certain that he has said as much of us behind our backs." William Jerdan practised Rogers-like qualification or rescinding: "I have used the word *friend* but it did not appear that the nonagenarian (whatever he might have enjoyed half a century before) had any friends. I never saw about him any but acquaintances or toadies." Presumably Jerdan never saw about himself any reason to fear that he'd be lumped among the latter.

Slily denigratory, condescending and cosseted, Rogers was a man of independent means – meaning that money depended to him by inheritance – and this with what is often a consequence of such good fortune: a lack of independent ends. A banker, he banked on his wealth to bring him into a world – political, literary, gossipy – that he lordlily slighted, serpentinely envied, and (it must be granted with gratitude) perceptively penetrated. It has to be said that he was very good at hearing what was said. Socially, he had not only his wits but his ears about him, everywhere about him. He put things down, often somebody's putting somebody down.

He was not himself a delight, but the jottings of this much-deferred-to man remain a delight.

His first editor, Alexander Dyce, was no mincer of words, though the following words of his did not figure in the publication:

The face and figure of Rogers were very peculiar. Though he had a fine ample forehead, his eyes were heavy and lustreless, his under-jaw was too prominent, his chin of more than ordinary length, and his complexion deadly pale. He was of the middle size, and strongly built; but ill-made in the lower limbs, and so awkward and shambling in his gait, that he sometimes attracted the notice of strangers in the street: yet in his youth he had been fond of dancing, and talked with pleasure of having had Miss De Camp (Mrs. Charles Kemble) for his partner at dancing parties given by Mrs. Siddons when she lived in Gt. Marlbro' Street; nay, at a much later period, he danced with Queen Caroline at Kensington Palace, and did not foot it with sufficient quickness to satisfy that undignified piece of royalty.

Miss De Camp! Nay! To satisfy! Piece of – ah – royalty!

He never married.

Dyce characterized what "was undoubtedly the effect of intercourse with Mr. Rogers, it was indeed improving". The posthumous publication of the notebook-entries improved in several respects when the edition of 1856 (the year after Rogers's death) gave way to that of 1859. The history is odd, in that the later – the leaner and better – of the two editions has the air of being the earlier. The earlier one, *Recollections of the Table-Talk of Samuel Rogers. To which is added Porsoniana* (London: Edward Moxon, 1856), is a self-important book of 350 pages. The self-importance is remittingly Rogers's and unremittingly that of the editor, the violently disputatious Alexander Dyce. The brief biographical preface ended with an assurance:

From my first introduction to Mr. Rogers, I was in the habit of writing down, in all their minutiæ, the anecdotes, &c. with which his conversation abounded: and once on my telling him that I did so, he expressed himself pleased, – the rather, perhaps, because he sometimes had the mortification of finding impatient listeners. Of those memoranda, which gradually accumulated to a large mass, a selection is contained in the following pages; the subjects being arranged (as far as such miscellaneous matter would admit of arrangement) under distinct heads; and nothing having been inserted which was likely to hurt the feelings of the living. A. D.

This report hurt the feelings of the living rivals for the continued favour of Rogers's company. Dyce's self-serving self-pleasing account ("he expressed himself pleased") failed to carry conviction in certain quarters, and he was promptly set upon. "Nor is Mr. Hamilton Gray the only person who has charged me with misrepresenting the conversation of Mr. Rogers." The preface to the 3rd edition concludes its eight pages of aggressive self-defence by declaring what it cannot conclude without:

I cannot conclude without noticing the insinuations which (in spite of what I said in the Preface to the first edition) have been thrown out from more than one quarter, that my memoranda of Mr. Rogers's conversation were hastily made towards the close of his life, when his memory was greatly impaired. Nothing can be farther from the truth: – they were every one of them written down at various times during a period which terminated at least five years before the death of Mr. Rogers. A. DYCE

Three years after Dyce's publication, there appeared a more modest book, physically modest too, smaller pages, and fewer of them: *Recollections* by Samuel Rogers (London: Longman, Brown, Green, Longmans, and Roberts, 1859). Making no mention of Dyce's ample spread, *Recollections* was edited by Rogers's nephew William Sharpe, with the name, the address, and the date – Highbury Terrace, May, 1859 – subscribed at the end of an unexclamatory Notice by the Editor.

Dyce had included much that was not to figure in Sharpe, but a good many of Dyce's pages
are no longer called for: very extensive quotations
from the poems and prose of Rogers himself and of
other people, dilatory narrative, and the like. Where
Dyce had a running sprawling sequence, Sharpe
respects the personable allocations that Rogers ap-
parently favoured, with Charles James Fox, Edmund
Burke, Henry Grattan and the others each enjoying
a run of pages. The present selection follows Sharpe
not only in this allocating but in its wording, for
Sharpe was right to value "the extreme concise-
ness", "that concise and colloquial style in which
Mr. Rogers delighted to write his Journals". Sharpe
catches a glint, a glancing; Dyce has a laboured way
of recounting, dilating, and dulling. Sharpe cocks
his ear, or rather Fox's:

*Gibbon a great coxcomb – his portrait by Sir Joshua
Reynolds is over the fire-place at Lausanne, and he used
to look at it as often as if it had been his mistress's. –*

Dyce sounds as though he prefers the sound of his
own voice:

*every now and then, too, casting a look of compla-
cency on his own portrait by Sir Joshua Reynolds,
which hung over the chimney-piece, – that wonderful
portrait, in which while the oddness and vulgarity of*

the features are refined away, the likeness is perfectly preserved.

But Dyce has to be called upon whenever Sharpe is unforthcoming, so the arrangement followed here is to begin with a section SAMUEL ROGERS, deploying a selection of the items that are to be found in Dyce alone, and then turning to the Sharpe pages with their individualities (given in alphabetical order): EDMUND BURKE, CHARLES JAMES FOX, HENRY GRATTAN, LORD GRENVILLE, RICHARD PORSON, TALLEYRAND, JOHN HORNE TOOKE, and the DUKE OF WELLINGTON.

The Index of Names incorporates brief annotations.

from NOTICE BY THE EDITOR
[William Sharpe, 1859]

The Recollections which form the contents of the present volume were left by Mr. Rogers in manuscript, but in a state which showed they were intended for publication.

It appears that from his first entering into society he noted down the conversation or remarks of those among his intimate friends in whose company he took the greatest pleasure; and subsequently, as these notes increased, and he felt they might become generally interesting, he proceeded, from time to time, to extract and collect those parts which he thought most worthy of perusal by others.

In some cases the selection of the materials, though begun by him, was left incomplete at his death. He had, however, pointed out by memoranda the names of the Individuals whose conversation he intended should form the collection, and the order in which they should stand.

There is an entry in his Note Book, in his own handwriting, in the following words: "Fox, Burke, Grattan, Porson, Tooke, Talleyrand, Erskine, Walter Scott, Lord Grenville, Duke of Wellington." By this and numerous other indications he has sufficiently shown the course he wished should be followed; and a short preface, written by him as an introduction to the Recollections, makes clear his intentions that they should not always remain unpublished.

Of the persons above named, Mr. Burke was the only one with whom Mr. Rogers was not intimately acquainted, and whose conversation was not taken down by him from personal communication. He knew Mr. Burke as a public man, and was indebted to friends for the Recollections of him included in this work.

With a view of rendering these Memorials as valuable as circumstances will allow, as well as of carrying out Mr. Rogers's apparent design, the Editor has, in addition to the extracts which he found already made from the Diaries, selected some further passages in connection with the persons named which appear of sufficient interest to be preserved, and which had probably been omitted owing to the extracts not having been completed. In doing this it is possible he has introduced some parts which Mr. Rogers might not have thought important enough to be put in print. It is hoped, however, that the Reader will not complain of the introduction of a few sentences which the Author may have left out, through accident or extreme caution; but to which the lapse of time has now given a value. The most extensive of the additions so made are the anecdotes of Burke by Dr. Lawrence, and a few of the miscellaneous remarks by the Duke of Wellington at p. 216 [here p.127] and the following pages.

Mr. Rogers, at times, no doubt intended that the Recollections should be published in his lifetime, and perhaps at a period when some of the persons described were living. Accidental circumstances, or further consideration, however, prevented the fulfilment of this intention; and caused him to leave to his Executors the agreeable task of laying these pages before the public: a pleasure which has been kindly yielded to the Editor by his Brother and Co-executor [Samuel Sharpe]. The Editor therefore feels that by the course he is now taking, he is only discharging a duty which he owes to the deceased; and he believes that the death of all the parties whose conversation is recorded, and the distance, in time, of the events described will justify the introduction of more than could be so well admitted at an earlier period.

PREFACE

[by Samuel Rogers]

Lord Clarendon was often heard to say that, next to the bless-
ing of almighty God, he owed all the little he knew and the
little good that was in him to the friendships and conversation
of the most excellent men; and he always charged his children
to follow his example; protesting that in the whole course of
his life he never knew one man, of what condition soever,
arrive at any degree of reputation in the world, who delighted
in the company of those who were not superior to himself.
– CLARENDON'S *Memoirs of his own Life.*[1]

 That such has been my practice through life, if not with
the same success, these pages can testify. By many they will
be thought of little value; but some may think otherwise. The
principal speakers here were men most eminent in their day;
the transactions in which they bore a part have now become
history; and some, who were then unborn, may not be unwilling to pass an hour or two in their company, to hear them
talk as they did, when they were most at their ease – in a
morning-walk or in an evening by the fire-side – and to share
what so few, even of their contemporaries, had the privilege
of enjoying.

1. Abridged from a passage in the Life of Lord Clarendon, written by
himself, 3rd edit. vol. I. p. 29.

– Samuel Rogers –

I was taught by my mother, from my earliest infancy, to be tenderly kind towards the meanest living thing; and, however people may laugh, I sometimes very carefully put a stray gnat or wasp out at the window. – My friend Lord Holland, though a kind-hearted man, does not mind killing flies and wasps; he says, "I have no feeling for *insects*." – When I was on the Continent with Richard Sharp we one day observed a woman amusing her child by holding what we at first thought was a mouse tied to a string, with which a cat was playing. Sharp was all indignation at the sight; till, on looking more closely, he found that the supposed mouse was a small rat; upon which he exclaimed, "Oh, I have no pity for *rats!*"

I can hardly persuade myself that there is no compensation in a future existence for the sufferings of animals in the present life, – for instance, when I see a horse in the streets unmercifully flogged by its brutal driver.

I well remember one of the heads of the rebels upon a pole at Temple-Bar, – a black shapeless lump. Another pole was bare, the head having dropt from it. [*"The last heads which remained on the Bar were those of Fletcher and Townley. 'Yesterday,' says a news-writer of the 1st of April 1772, 'one of the rebels' heads on Temple Bar fell down. There is only one head now remaining.'"* Ed., 1856]

When I was a school-boy, I wore, like other school-boys, a cocked hat; – we used to run about the fields, chasing butterflies, in cocked hats. After growing up, I have walked through St. Paul's Churchyard in a cocked hat.

I saw Garrick act only once, – the part of Ranger in *The Suspicious Husband*. I remember that there was a great crowd, and that we waited long in a dark passage of the theatre, on our way to the pit. I was then a little boy. My father had promised to take me to see Garrick in Lear; but a fit of the mumps kept me at home.

Before his going abroad, Garrick's attraction had much decreased; Sir William Weller Pepys said that the pit was often almost empty. But, on his return to England, people were mad about seeing him; and Sir George Beaumont and several others used frequently to get admission into the pit, before the doors were opened to the public, by means of bribing the attendants, who bade them "be sure, as soon as the crowd rushed in, to pretend to be in a great heat, and to wipe their faces, as if they had just been struggling for entrance."

Dr. Johnson said to an acquaintance of mine, "My other works are wine and water; but my *Rambler* is pure wine." The world now thinks differently.

Lady Spencer recollected Johnson well, as she used to see him often in her girlhood. Her mother, Lady Lucan, would say, "Nobody dines with us to-day; therefore, child, we'll go and get Dr. Johnson." So they would drive to Bolt Court, and bring the doctor home with them.

By the by, General Fitzpatrick remembered the time when St. James's Street used to be crowded with the carriages of the ladies and gentlemen who were walking in the Mall, – the ladies with their heads in full dress, and the gentlemen carrying their hats under their arms. The proprietors of Ranelagh and Vauxhall used to send decoy-ducks among them, that is, persons attired in the height of fashion, who every now and then would exclaim in a very audible tone, "What charming weather for Ranelagh" or "for Vauxhall!"

Ranelagh was a very pleasing place of amusement. There persons of inferior rank mingled with the highest nobility of Britain. All was so orderly and still, that you could hear the *whishing* sound of the ladies' trains, as the immense assembly walked round and round the room. If you chose, you might have tea, which was served up in the neatest equipage possible. The price of admission was half-a-crown. People generally went to Ranelagh between nine and ten o'clock.

What a quantity of snuff Sir Joshua took! I once saw him at an Academy-dinner, when his waistcoat was absolutely powdered with it.

Sir Joshua was always thinking of his art. He was one day walking with Dr. Lawrence near Beaconsfield, when they met a beautiful little peasant-boy. Sir Joshua, after looking earnestly at the child, exclaimed, "I must go home and deepen the colouring of my *Infant Hercules*." The boy was a good deal sun-burnt.

I can hardly believe what was told me long ago by a gentleman living in the Temple, who, however, assured me that it was fact. He happened to be passing by Sir Joshua's house in Leicester Square, when he saw a poor girl seated on the steps and crying bitterly. He asked what was the matter; and she replied that she was crying "because *the one shilling* which she had received from Sir Joshua for sitting to him as a model, had proved to be a bad one, and he would not give her another."

I recollect when it was still the fashion for gentlemen to wear swords. I have seen Haydn play at a concert in a tie-wig, with a sword at his side.

Doctor Fordyce sometimes drank a good deal at dinner. He was summoned one evening to see a lady patient, when he was more than half-seas-over, and conscious that he was so. Feeling her pulse, and finding himself unable to count its beats, he muttered, "Drunk, by God!" Next morning, recollecting the circumstances, he was greatly vexed: and just as he was thinking what explanation of his behaviour he should offer to the lady, a letter from her was put into his hand. "She too well knew," said the letter, "that he had discovered the unfortunate condition in which she was when he last visited her; and she entreated him to keep the matter secret in consideration of the enclosed (a hundred-pound bank-note)."

People are now so fond of *the obscure* in poetry, that they can perceive no *deep thinking* in that darling man Pope, because he always expresses himself with such admirable clearness.

I sometimes wonder how a man can ever be cheerful, when he knows that he *must* die. But what poets write about *the horrors of the grave* makes not the slightest impression upon me; for instance what Dryden says;

"Vain men! how vanishing a bliss we crave!
Now warm in love, now withering in the grave!
Never, O, never more, to see the sun,
Still dark, in a damp vault, and still alone!"

All this is unphilosophical; in fact, nonsense. The body, when the soul has left it, is as worthless as an old garment, – rather more so, for it rots much sooner.

Sir George Beaumont, when a young man, was one day in the Mount (a famous coffee-house in Mount Street, Grosvenor Square) with Hervey Aston. Various persons were seated at different tables. Among others present, there was an Irishman who was very celebrated as a duellist, having killed at least half-a-dozen antagonists. Aston, talking to some of his acquaintance, swore that he would make the duellist stand barefooted before them. "You had better take care what you say," they replied; "he has his eye upon you." – 'No matter," rejoined Aston; "I declare again that he shall stand barefooted before you, if you will make up among you a purse of fifty guineas." They did so. Aston then said in a loud voice, "I have been in Ireland, and am well acquainted with the natives." The Irishman was all ear. Aston went on, "The Irish, being born in bogs, are every one of them web-footed; I know it for a fact." –"Sir," roared the duellist, starting up from his table, "it is false!" Aston persisted in his assertion. "Sir," cried the other, "*I* was born in Ireland; and I will prove to you that it is a falsehood." So saying, in great haste he pulled off his shoes and stockings, and displayed his bare feet. The joke ended in Aston's sharing the purse between the Irishman and himself, giving the former thirty guineas, and keeping twenty. Sir George assured me that this was a true story.

At Brighton, during my youth, I became acquainted with a lawyer who had known Gray. He said that Gray's pronunciation was very affected, *e.g.* "What *naise* (noise) is that?"

Henley [the translator of Beckford's *Vathek*] was one morning paying a visit to Gray, when a dog came into the room. "Is that your dog?" said Henley. "No," replied Gray: "do you suppose that *I* would keep an animal *by which I might possibly lose my life?*"

I once read Gray's *Ode to Adversity* to Wordsworth;
and at the line, –

"And leave us leisure to be good,"–
Wordsworth exclaimed, "I am quite sure *that* is not
original; Gray could not have hit upon it."
[*The Rev. J. Mitford, in his ed. of Gray, cites ad l.,
"And know, I have not yet* the leisure to be good."
Oldham, Ode, *st. 5.* ED., 1856]

It is Gray, I think, who somewhere says that monosyllables should be avoided in poetry: but there are
many lines consisting only of monosyllables, which
could not possibly be improved. For instance, in
Shakespeare's *Romeo and Juliet*, –

"Thou canst not speak of what thou dost not feel;"
and in Pope's *Eloisa to Abelard*, –

"Pant on thy lip, and to thy heart be prest;
Give all thou canst, and let me dream the rest."

Topham Beauclerk (Johnson's friend) was a strangely
absent person. One day he had a party coming to
dinner; and, just before their arrival, he went up-
stairs to change his dress. He forgot all about them;
thought that it was bed-time, pulled off his clothes,
and got into bed. A servant, who presently entered
the room to tell him that his guests were waiting for
him, found him fast asleep.

At a dinner-party in Paris, given by a French noble-
man, I saw a black bottle of English porter set on the
table as a great rarity, and drunk out of small glasses.

Boddington had a wretchedly bad memory; and, in
order to improve it, he attended Feinaigle's lectures
on the Art of Memory. Soon after, somebody asked
Boddington the name of the lecturer; and, for his
life, he could not recollect it. –When I was asked
if I had attended the said lectures on the Art of
Memory, I replied, "No: I wished to learn the Art
of Forgetting."

He [John Wilkes] was quite as ugly, and squinted
as much, as his portraits make him; but he was very
gentlemanly in appearance and manners. I think I
see him at this moment, walking through the crowded streets of the city, as Chamberlain, on his way
to Guildhall, in a scarlet coat, military boots, and a
bag-wig, – the hackney-coachmen in vain calling out
to him, "A coach, your honour?"

Words are so twisted and tortured by some writers
of the present day, that I am really sorry for them, – I
mean, for the words. It is a favourite fancy of mine
that perhaps in the next world the use of words may
be dispensed with, – that our thoughts may stream

into each others' minds without any verbal communication.

Parr often spoke with much bitterness of Mackintosh: among other severe things, he said that "Mackintosh came up from Scotland with a metaphysical head, a cold heart, and open hands."

He [Parr] had a horror of the east wind; and Tom Sheridan once kept him prisoner in the house for a fortnight by fixing the weathercock in that direction.

We have far better tragic writers than Corneille or Racine; but we have no one to be compared with Moliére, – no one *like* him.

When she [Helen Maria Williams] was in Paris, during the Revolution, she had seen men and women, who were waiting for admission at the door of the theatre, suddenly leave their station on the passing of a set of wretches going to be guillotined, and then, after having ascertained that none of their relations or friends were among them, very unconcernedly return to the door of the theatre.

When Lord Erskine heard that somebody had died worth two hundred thousand pounds, he observed,

"Well, that's a very pretty sum to begin the next world with."

"A friend of mine," said Erskine, "was suffering from a continual wakefulness; and various methods were tried to send him to sleep, but in vain. At last his physicians resorted to an experiment which succeeded perfectly: they dressed him in a watchman's coat, put a lantern into his hand, placed him in a sentry-box, and – he was asleep in ten minutes."

To all letters soliciting his "subscription" to any thing, Erskine had a regular form of reply, viz. "Sir, I feel much honoured by your application to me, and I beg to subscribe" – here the reader had to turn over the leaf – "myself your very ob^t servant," &c.

Erskine used to say that when the hour came that all secrets should be revealed, we should know the reason why – shoes are always made too tight.

Dunning (afterwards Lord Ashburton) was "stating the law" to a jury at Guildhall, when Lord Mansfield interrupted him by saying, "If *that* be law, I'll go home and burn my books." – "My Lord," replied Dunning, "you had better go home and *read* them."

Dunning was remarkably ugly. One night, while he was playing whist, at Nando's, with Horne Tooke and two others, Lord Thurlow called at the door, and desired the waiter to give a note to Dunning (with whom, though their politics were so different, he was very intimate). The waiter did not know Dunning by sight. "Take the note up stairs," said Thurlow, "and deliver it to the ugliest man at the card-table – to him who most resembles the knave of spades." The note immediately reached its destination.

I was present on the second day of Hastings's trial in Westminster Hall; when Sheridan was listened to with such attention that you might have heard a pin drop. – During one of those days Sheridan, having observed Gibbon among the audience, took occasion to mention "the luminous author of *The Decline and Fall*." After he had finished, one of his friends reproached him with flattering Gibbon. "Why, what did I say of him?" asked Sheridan. – "You called him the luminous author," &c. – "Luminous! oh, I meant – *v*oluminous."

[*But, as reported in* The Morning Chronicle, *June 14, 1788, the expression used by Sheridan was "The correct periods of Tacitus or the* luminous *page of Gibbon." – "Before my departure from England, I was present at the august spectacle of Mr. Hastings's trial in Westminster Hall. It is not my province to absolve or condemn the Governor of India; but Mr. Sheridan's eloquence demanded my applause; nor could I hear without emotion the personal compliment which he paid me in the presence of the British nation." Gibbon's Memoirs, &c.* ED., 1856]

When the Duke of York was obliged to retreat before the French, Sheridan gave as a toast, "The Duke of York and his brave followers."

Sheridan had very fine eyes, and he was not a little vain of them. He said to me on his death-bed, "Tell Lady Bessborough that my eyes will look up to the coffin-lid as brightly as ever."

In his dealings with the world, Sheridan certainly carried the *privileges of genius* as far as they were ever carried by man.

It is quite true, as stated in several accounts of him, that Fox, when a very young man, was a prodigious dandy, – wearing a little odd French hat, shoes with red heels, &c. He and Lord Carlisle once traveled from Paris to Lyons for the express purpose of buying waistcoats; and during the whole journey they talked about nothing else.

Fox (in his earlier days, I mean), Sheridan, Fitzpatrick, &c., led *such* a life! Lord Tankerville assured me that he has played cards with Fitzpatrick at Brookes's from ten o'clock at night till near six o'clock the next afternoon, a waiter standing by to tell them "whose deal it was," they being too sleepy to know.

After losing large sums at hazard, Fox would go home, – not to destroy himself, as his friends sometimes feared, but – to sit down quietly, and read Greek.

He once won about eight thousand pounds; and one of his bond-creditors, who soon heard of his good luck, presented himself, and asked for payment. "Impossible, sir," replied Fox; "I must first discharge my debts of honour." The bond-creditor remonstrated. "Well, sir, give me your bond." It was delivered to Fox, who tore it in pieces and threw them into the fire. "Now, sir," said Fox, "my debt to you is a debt of honour;" and immediately paid him.

In London mixed society Fox conversed little; but at his own house in the country, with his intimate friends, he would talk on for ever, with all the openness and simplicity of a child: he has continued talking to me for half-an-hour after he had taken up his bed-room candle.

Pitt's voice sounded as if he had worsted in his mouth.

Fox once said to me that "Burke was a most impracticable person, a most unmanageable colleague, – that he never would support any measure, however convinced he might be in his heart of its utility, if it had been first proposed by another."

A natural son of Fox, a dumb boy (who was the very image of his father, and who died a few years after, when about the age of fifteen) was also there, having come, for the occasion, from Braidwood's Academy. To him Fox almost entirely confined his attention, conversing with him by the fingers; and their eyes glistened as they looked at each other. Talleyrand remarked to me, "how strange it was to dine in company with the first orator in Europe, and only see him *talk with his fingers!*"

At a dinner-party, where I was, Fox met Aikin. "I am greatly pleased with your *Miscellaneous Pieces*, Mr. Aikin," said Fox (alluding to the volume written partly by Aikin, and partly by his sister Mrs. Barbauld). Aikin bowed. "I particularly admire," continued Fox, "your essay *Against Inconsistency in our Expectations*." "That," replied Aikin, "is my sister's." – "I like much," resumed Fox, "your essay *On Monastic Institutions*." "That," answered Aikin, "is also my sister's." Fox thought it best to say no more about the book.

I saw Lunardi make the first ascent in a balloon which had been witnessed in England. It was from the Artillery Ground. Fox was there with his brother General F. The crowd was immense. Fox, happening to put his hand down to his watch, found another hand upon it, which he immediately seized. "My friend," said he to the owner of the strange hand, "you have chosen an occupation which will be your ruin at last." "O, Mr. Fox," was the reply, "forgive me, and let me go! I have been driven to this course by necessity alone; my wife and children are starving at home." Fox, always tender-hearted, slipped a guinea into the hand, and then released it. On the conclusion of the show, Fox was proceeding to look what o'clock it was. "Good God," cried he "my watch is gone!" "Yes," answered General F., "I know it is; I saw your friend take it." – "Saw him take it! and you made no attempt to stop him?" "Really, you and he appeared to be on such good terms with each other, that I did not choose to interfere."

Most unfortunately, one morning during breakfast at St. Ann's Hill, I repeated and praised Goldsmith's song, "When lovely woman stoops to folly," &c., quite forgetting that it must necessarily hurt the feelings of Mrs. Fox. She seemed a good deal discomposed by it. Fox merely remarked, "Some people write damned nonsense."

He was an eager chess-player: I have heard him say, on coming down to breakfast, that he had not been able to sleep for thinking about some particular move.

I introduced Wordsworth to Fox, having taken him with me to a ball given by Mrs. Fox. "I am very glad to see you, Mr. Wordsworth, though I am not of your faction," was all that Fox said to him, – meaning that he admired a school of poetry different from that to which Wordsworth belonged.

One forenoon, at his own house, Fox was talking to me very earnestly about Dryden, when he suddenly recollected that (being in office) he ought to make his appearance at the King's levee. It was so late that, not having time to change his dress, he set off for court "accoutred as he was;" and when somebody remarked to him that his coat was not quite the thing, he replied, "No matter; *he* [i.e. George the Third] is

so blind that he can't distinguish what I have on."
Very shortly before he died, he complained of great
uneasiness in his stomach; and Cline advised him
to try the effects of a cup of coffee. It was accord-
ingly ordered: but, not being brought so soon as
was expected, Mrs. Fox expressed some impatience;
upon which Fox said, with his usual sweet smile,
"Remember, my dear, that good coffee cannot be
made in a moment."

Lady Holland announced the death of Fox in her
own odd manner to those relatives and intimate
friends of his who were sitting in a room near his
bed-chamber, and waiting to hear that he had
breathed his last; − she walked through the room
with her apron thrown over her head.

Lord St. Helens also told me that he and Ségur were
with the Empress [Catherine] in her carriage, when
the horses took fright, and ran furiously down the
hill. The danger was excessive. When it was over,
the Empress said, "Mon étoile vous a sauvée."

Fitzpatrick, who had been much in the company of
David Hume, used always to speak of him as "a deli-
cious creature."

Towards the close of his life, till he received a pension

of 200*l.* per annum from the king, Murphy was in great pecuniary difficulties. He had eaten himself out of every tavern from the other side of Temple-Bar to the west end of the town.

Murphy used to say that there were Four Estates in England, the King, the Lords, the Commons, and – *the Theatres.* He certainly would not say so, if he were alive now, when the national theatre is almost extinct.

During his boyhood, Pitt was very weakly; and his physician, Addington (Lord Sidmouth's father), ordered him to take port wine in large quantities: the consequence was, that, when he grew up, he could not do without it. Lord Grenville has seen him swallow a bottle of port in tumblerfuls, before going to the House. This, together with his habit of eating late suppers (indigestible cold veal-pies, &c.), helped undoubtedly to shorten his life. Huskisson, speaking to me of Pitt, said that his hands shook so much, that, when he helped himself to salt, he was obliged to support the right hand with the left.

I recollect a farmer coming to my father's bank, and receiving his money in five-pound notes. "What can I do with these?" he exclaimed; "how can I pay my men with them?"

[*Very shortly before this (as my friend Mr. Samuel Sharpe informs me) five-pound notes had been issued: smaller notes were not issued till some time afterwards.* ED., 1856]

Gibbon took very little exercise. He had been staying some time with Lord Sheffield in the country; and when he was about to go away, the servants could not find his hat. "Bless me," said Gibbon, "I certainly left it in the hall on my arrival here." He had not stirred out of doors during the whole of the visit.

Lord Chesterfield remarked of two persons dancing a minuet, that "they looked as if they were hired to do it, and were doubtful of being paid."

I once observed to a Scotch lady, "how desirable it was in any danger *to have presence of mind*." "I had rather," she rejoined, "*have absence of body*."

I paid five guineas (in conjunction with Boddington) for a *loge* at Tooke's trial. – It was the custom in those days (and perhaps is so still) to place bunches of strong-smelling plants of different sorts at the bar where the criminal was to sit (I suppose, to purify the air from the contagion of his presence!). This was done at Tooke's trial; but, as soon as he was brought in, he indignantly swept them away with his handkerchief. The trial lasted six days. Erskine (than whom nobody had ever more power over a jury, – he would frequently address them as "his little twelvers") defended Tooke most admirably: nay, he showed himself not only a great orator, but a great actor; for, on the fifth day, when the Attorney-General, Eldon, was addressing the jury, and was using a line of argument which Erskine had not expected and could not reply to (the pleading for the prisoner being closed), I well remember how Erskine the whole time kept turning towards the jury, and by a series of significant looks, shrugs, and shakings of his head, did all he could to destroy the effect of what the Attorney-General was saying.

Vernon was the person who invented the story about the lady being pulverized in India by a *coup de soleil*: – when he was dining there with a Hindoo, one of his host's wives was suddenly reduced to ashes; upon which, the Hindoo *rang the bell*, and said to the attendant who answered it, "Bring fresh glasses, and sweep up your mistress."

Another of his stories was this. He happened to be shooting hyenas near Carthage, when he stumbled, and fell down an abyss of many fathoms' depth. He was surprised, however, to find himself unhurt; for he lighted as if on a feather-bed. Presently he perceived that he was gently moved upwards; and, having by degrees reached the mouth of the abyss, he again stood safe on *terra firma*. He had fallen upon an immense mass of bats, which, disturbed from their slumbers, had risen out of the abyss and brought him up with them.

Steevens once said to Mathias, "Well, sir, since you deny the authorship of *The Pursuits of Literature*, I need have no hesitation in declaring to you that the person who wrote it is a liar and a blackguard."

Lane made a large fortune by the immense quantity of trashy novels which he sent forth from his Minerva-press. I perfectly well remember the splendid carriage in which he used to ride, and his footmen with their cockades and gold-headed canes. Now-a-days, as soon as a novel has had its run, and is beginning to be forgotten, out comes an edition of it as a "standard novel"!

Lord Nelson was a remarkably kind-hearted man. I have seen him spin a teetotum with his *one* hand, a whole evening, for the amusement of some children.

A person once asserted that in a particular country the bees were as large as sheep. He was asked "How big, then, are the hives?" – "Oh," he replied, "the usual size."

In Milton's description of the lazar-house there is a dreadful confusion of metaphor: –

> "Sight so deform what *heart of rock* could long
>   *Dry-ey'd* behold?"

I once observed this to Coleridge, who told Wordsworth that he could not sleep all the next night for thinking of it.

It is remarkable that no poet before Shakespeare ever introduced a person *walking in sleep*. I believe there is no allusion to such a circumstance in any of the Greek or Latin poets.

If you wish to have your works *coldly* reviewed, get your intimate friend to write an article on them. I know this by experience.

Sir Henry Englefield had a fancy (which some greater men have had) that there was about his person a natural odour of roses and violets. Lady Grenville, hearing of this, and loving a joke, exclaimed, one day when Sir Henry was present, "Bless me, what a smell of violets!" – "Yes," said he with great simplicity; "it comes from me."

As to Flaxman, the greatest sculptor of his day, – the

neglect which *he* experienced is something inconceivable. Canova, who was well acquainted with his exquisite illustrations of Dante, &c., could hardly believe that a man of such genius was not an object of admiration among his countrymen; and, in allusion to their insensibility to Flaxman's merits and to their patronage of inferior artists, he said to some of the English at Rome, "*You* see with your ears!"

Grattan said that Malone went about, looking, through strongly-magnifying spectacles, for pieces of straw and bits of broken glass.

"Do you ever say your prayers?" asked Plunket of Grattan. "No, never." – "What, never! neither night nor morning?" "Never: but I have aspirations all day long."

"What you have just mentioned," said one of Grattan's friends to him, "is a profound secret: where *could* you have heard it?" Grattan replied, "Where secrets are kept, – in the street."

The French Revolution was the greatest event in Europe since the irruption of the Goths.

Archibald Hamilton, afterwards Duke of Hamilton, (as his daughter, Lady Dunmore, told me) advertised for "a Hermit" as an ornament to his pleasure-grounds; and it was stipulated that the said Hermit should have his beard shaved but once a year, and that only partially.

A friend, calling on him one forenoon, asked if it was true that he kept a young tame tiger. He immediately slapped his thighs, and uttered a sort of whistle; and forth crept the long-backed animal from under the sofa. The visitor soon retreated.

Lord Shelburne could say the most provoking things, and yet appear quite unconscious of their being so. In one of his speeches, alluding to Lord Carlisle, he said, "The noble lord has written a comedy." "No, a tragedy." – "Oh, I beg pardon; *I thought it was a comedy.*"

Only look at that sunset! it is enough to make one feel devout.

Once at Thomas Grenville's house I was rapturously admiring a sunset. "Yes," he observed, "it is very *handsome*:" and some time after, when — was admiring another sunset, he said, "Why, you are as foolish as Rogers."

When a lady, a friend of mine, was in Italy, she went

into a church, and knelt down among the crowd. An Italian woman, who was praying at some little distance, rose up, came softly to my friend, whispered in her ear, "If you continue to flirt with my husband, I'll be the death of you;" and then, as softly, returned to her genuflections. Such things cannot happen where there are pews.

When I was a lad, I recollect seeing a whole cartful of girls, in dresses of various colours, on their way to be executed at Tyburn. They had all been condemned, on one indictment, for having been concerned in (that is, perhaps, for having been spectators of) the burning of some houses during Lord George Gordon's riots. It was quite horrible. – Greville was present at one of the trials consequent on those riots, and heard several boys sentenced, to their own excessive amazement, to be hanged. "Never," said Greville with great *naïveté*, "did I see boys *cry so*."

When Kemble was living at Lausanne, he used to feel rather jealous of Mont Blanc; he disliked to hear people always asking, "How does Mont Blanc look this morning?"

The English highwaymen of former days (indeed, the race is now extinct) were remarkably well-bred personages. Thomas Grenville, while travelling with

Lord Derby; and Lord Tankerville, while travelling with his father; were attacked by highwaymen: on both occasions, six or seven shots were exchanged between them and the highwaymen; and when the parties assailed had expended all their ammunition, the highwaymen came up to them, and took their purses in the politest manner possible.

Such is the eagerness of the human mind for excitement, – for *an event*, – that people generally have a sort of satisfaction in reading the deaths of their friends in the newspapers. I don't mean that a man would not be shocked to read there the death of his child, or of his dearest friend; but that he feels a kind of pleasure in reading that of an acquaintance, because it gives him something to talk about with every body on whom he may have to call during the day.

George Selwyn, as every body knows, delighted in seeing executions; he never missed *being in at a death* at Tyburn. When Lord Holland (the father of Charles Fox) was confined to bed by a dangerous illness, he was informed by his servant that Mr. Selwyn had recently called to inquire for him. "On his next visit," said Lord Holland, "be sure you let him in, whether I am alive or a corpse; for, if I am alive, *I* shall have great pleasure in seeing *him*; and if *I* am a corpse, *he will have great pleasure in seeing me.*"

In all his domestic relations Southey was the most amiable of men; but he had no general philanthropy; he was what you call *a cold man*. He was never happy except when reading a book or making one.

Bishop Horsley one day met Monsey in the Park. "These are dreadful times!" said Horsley: "not only do deists abound, but, – would you think it, doctor? – some people deny that there is a God!" "I can tell you," replied Monsey, "what is equally strange, – some people believe that there are three." Horsley immediately walked away.

A certain man of pleasure about London received a challenge from a young gentleman of his acquaintance; and they met at the appointed place. Just before the signal for firing was given, the man of pleasure rushed up to his antagonist, embraced him, and vehemently protested that "he could not lift his arm *against his own flesh and blood!*" The young gentleman, though he had never heard any imputation cast upon his mother's character, was so much staggered, that (as the ingenious man of pleasure had foreseen) no duel took place.

Lord Alvanley on returning home, after his duel with young O'Connel, gave a guinea to the hackney-coachman who had driven him out and brought him back. The man, surprised at the largeness of the sum, said, "My lord, I only took you to —" Alvanley interrupted him, "My friend, the guinea is *for bringing me back*, not for taking me out."

Beckford read to me the two unprinted episodes to *Vathek*; and they are extremely fine, but very objectionable on account of their subjects. Indeed, they show that the mind of the author was to a certain degree diseased. The one is the story of a prince and princess, a brother and a sister. * * * * The other is the tale of a prince who is violently enamoured of a lady; and who, after pursuing her through various countries, at last overtakes her only to find her a corpse. * * * * In one of these tales there is an exquisite description of a voyage down the Nile.

To any one who has reached a very advanced age, a walk through the streets of London is like a walk in a cemetery. How many houses do I pass, now inhabited by strangers, in which I used to spend such happy hours with those who have long been dead and gone!

Most people are ever on the watch to find fault with

their children, and are afraid of *praising* them for fear of *spoiling* them. Now, I am sure that nothing has a better effect on children than *praise*. I had a proof of this in Moore's daughter: he used always to be saying to her, "What a *good* little girl!" and she continued to grow more and more good, till she became too good for this world, and died.

Latterly, I believe, Byron never dined with Lady B.; for it was one of his fancies (or affectations) that "he could not endure to see women eat."

My latest intercourse with Byron was in Italy. We travelled some time together; and, if there was any scenery particularly well worth seeing, he generally contrived that we should pass through it in the dark.

As we were crossing the Apennines, he told me that he had left an order in his will that Allegra, the child who soon after died, his daughter by Miss C., should never be taught the English language. − You know that Allegra was buried at Harrow: but probably you have not heard that the body was sent over to England in *two* packages, that no one might suspect what it was.

I went with him to see the Campo Santo at Pisa. It was shown to us by a man who had two handsome daughters. Byron told me that he had in vain paid his addresses to the elder daughter, but that he was on the most intimate terms with the other. Probably there was not one syllable of truth in all this; for he always had the weakness of wishing to be thought much worse than he really was.

Mrs. Barbauld once observed to me that *she* thought Byron wrote best when he wrote about the *sea* or *swimming*.

A lady resident in Aberdeen told me that she used to sit in a pew of St. Paul's Chapel in that town, next to Mrs. Byron's; and that one Sunday she observed the poet (then about seven or eight years old) amusing himself by disturbing his mother's devotions: he every now and then gently pricked with a pin the large round arms of Mrs. Byron, which were covered with white kid gloves.

The letters I receive from people, of both sexes (people whom I never heard of), asking me for money, either as a gift or as a loan, are really innumerable. Here's one from a student at Durham, requesting me to lend him 90*l*. (how modest to stop short of the hundred!). I lately had a begging epistle from a lady, who assured me that she used formerly to take evening walks with me in the Park: of course I did not answer it; and a day or two after, I had a second letter from her, beginning "Unkind one!"

I have heard Crabbe describe his mingled feelings of hope and fear as he stood on London Bridge, when he first came up to town to try his fortune in the literary world.

It is curious how fashion changes pronunciation. In my youth every body said "Lonnon," not "London:" Fox said "Lonnon" to the last; and so did Crowe. The now fashionable pronunciation of several words is to me at least very offensive: "cóntemplate" is bad enough; but "balcŏny" makes me sick."

I cannot forgive Goethe for certain things in his *Faust* and *Wilhelm Meister*: the man who appeals to the worst part of my nature commits a great offence.

The talking openly of their own merits is a "magnanimity" peculiar to foreigners.

This is not a bad charade: What is it that causes a cold, cures a cold, and pays the doctor? A draft.

He [William Stewart Rose] was in a sad state of mental imbecility shortly before his death. When people attempted to enter into conversation with him, he would continue to ask them two questions, "When did Sir Walter Scott die?" and "How is Lord Holland?" (who was already dead).

Once, when in company with William the Fourth, I quite forgot that it is against all etiquette to ask a sovereign about his health; and, on his saying to me, "Mr. Rogers, I hope you are well," I replied, "Very well, I thank your majesty: *I trust that your majesty is quite well also.*" Never was a king in greater confusion; he didn't know where to look, and stammered out, "Yes, − yes, − only a little rheumatism."

Dining one day with the Princess of Wales (Queen Caroline), I heard her say that on her first arrival in this country, she could speak only *one* word of English. Soon after, I mentioned that circumstance to a large party; and a discussion arose what English word would be most useful for a person to know, supposing that person's knowledge of the language must be limited to a single word. The greater number of the company fixed on "Yes." But Lady Charlotte Lindsay said that she should prefer "No;" because, though "Yes" never meant "No," − "No" very often meant "Yes."

One night, after dining with her [Queen Caroline]

at Kensington Palace, I was sitting in the carriage, waiting for Sir Henry Englefield to accompany me to town, when a sentinel, at about twenty yards' distance from me, was struck dead by a flash of lightning. I never beheld any thing like that flash: it was a body of flame, in the centre of which were quivering zigzag fires, such as artists put into the hand of Jupiter; and, after being visible for a moment, it seemed to explode. I immediately returned to the hall of the Palace, where I found the servants standing in terror, with their faces against the wall.

Nobody, I imagine, except a king, has any liking for a state bedchamber.

One day when George the Fourth was talking about his youthful exploits, he mentioned, with particular satisfaction, that he had made a body of troops charge down the Devil's Dyke (near Brighton). Upon which the Duke of Wellington merely observed to him, "Very steep, sir."

Dr. Lawrence assured me that Burke shortened his life by the frequent use of emetics, –"he was always tickling his throat with a feather." He complained of an oppression at his chest, which he fancied emetics would remove.

I often met Murat when he was on horseback, and he would invariably call out to me, rising in his stirrups, "Hé, monsieur, êtes-vous inspiré aujourdhui?"

What a disgusting thing is the *fagging* at our great schools! When Lord Holland was a schoolboy, he was forced, as a fag, to toast bread *with his fingers* for the breakfast of another boy. Lord H.'s mother sent him a toasting-fork. His fagger broke it over his head, and still compelled him to prepare the toast in the old way. In consequence of this process his fingers suffered so much that they always retained a withered appearance.

Lord Holland persisted in saying that pictures gave him more pain than pleasure. He also hated music; yet, in some respects, he had a very good ear, for he was a capital mimic.

Moore has now taken to an amusement which is very well suited to the fifth act of life; – he plays cribbage every night with Mrs. Moore.

Visiting Lady — one day, I made inquiries about her sister. "She is now staying with me," answered Lady —, "but she is unwell in consequence of a fright which she got on her way from Richmond to London." At that time omnibuses were great rarities; and while Miss — was coming to town, the footman, observing an omnibus approach, and thinking that she might like to see it, suddenly called in at the carriage-window, "Ma'am, the omnibus!" Miss —, being unacquainted with the term, and not sure but an *omnibus* might be a wild beast escaped from the Zoological Gardens, was thrown into a dreadful state of agitation by the announcement.

At one time, when I gave a dinner, I used to have candles placed all round the dining-room, and high up, in order to show off the pictures. I asked Sydney Smith how he liked that plan. "Not at all," he replied; "above, there is a blaze of light, and below, nothing but darkness and gnashing of teeth."

He said that — was so fond of contradiction, that he would throw up the window in the middle of the night, and contradict the watchman who was calling the hour.

When his physician advised him to "take a walk upon an empty stomach," Smith asked, "Upon whose?"

According to Smith, "Mr. —'s idea of heaven was eating *pâtés de foie gras* to the sound of trumpets."

[*"He alluded,"* as his daughter Lady Holland obligingly *informs me,* "to an eminent lawyer, who had a passion *for pâtés de foie gras (a passion in which Mr. Smith did* *not at all share), and who used to set off to purchase* *them as soon as the vacation permitted."*]

He said, "The Bishop of — is so like Judas, that I now firmly believe in the Apostolical Succession."

It was bed-time, when the captain of the vessel came to him, and said, "It will soon be all over with us." – "Very well," answered the Duke [of Wellington], "then I shall not take off my boots."

– Edmund Burke –

S omebody, who had met Mr. Fox abroad, mentioned his early attachment to France and French manners. Yes, said Mr. B., his attachment has been great, and long, and like a Cat, he has continued faithful to the house, after the family has left it.

Lord Chatham was a great Minister, and bold in his undertakings. He inspired the people with warlike ardour when it was necessary. He considered Mobs in the light of a raw material, which might be manufactured to a proper stuff for their own happiness in the end.

Dull Prosers are preferable to dull Jokers. The first require only patience; but the last harass the spirits, and check their spontaneous action.

More indulgence should be shown to Story-tellers. A story to be good, should be a little long sometimes; and in general, when a man offers you his story, it is the best thing he has to give you.

Emigrants. It is in human nature, as well as in brute nature, to dislike a fellow-creature in a state of degradation. Dogs will insult a dog with a canister at his tail, and when a boy, I have often played with other boys at a trick to cover one turkey with mud, that we might observe how other turkeys would tease it. Compassion, like every other feeling, may be worn out. He had a great indulgence for the prejudices which were against the Emigrants.

A great admirer of Swift's humour, particularly in his namby-pamby letters to Stella, which he always praised for their genuine gracefulness and ease. It being observed that many could not relish them in early life, but had grown to like them afterwards, he said: In early life we have generally a serious turn. It is in youth that the reasoning powers are strongest, though the stock is then too small to make any show with. The imagination becomes strongest after youth; for however ready it is to come forward, it cannot be exercised without a stock of knowledge.

England is, at all times, a moon shone upon by France. France contains all within herself. She has natural advantages; she can rise soon after severe blows. England is an artificial country. Take away her Commerce, what has she?

All colours are blended well by Gold. Gold is the colour of Light, and produces the effect of sunshine – our very language confesses the pleasure we derive from gilded objects. Many years ago Mrs. Fox lamented with me the loss of true taste in England on this point. Gilding was so much the taste of the Antients, that they gilded their favourite statues; and remains of it are seen on the Venus de Medici. She was sometimes styled Aurea Venus on this account. The Romans gilded their walls and ceilings more than the Greeks, because they had more Gold.

Good humour too often confounded with Good nature, which has a much less servile character.

Every farm held by a gentleman, is, in proportion to its magnitude, a loss. No gentleman can give his time and attention to such details as are necessary to minute economy, and which no farm can prosper without.

Burke sleeps but ill, and often rises at day-break; makes the tour of his farm, oversees his men at work, and then returns to bed. Walks in his fields with a spud in his hand, making war upon the nettles, and breaking the clods; and often makes a stop in conversation on the grandest topic to direct the lading of a dung cart.

After dinner he retires to a nap, but returns to tea, and when the card-table is set, retires again for three, four, or five hours.

In argument puts out his whole strength, but is ready to listen, and full of inquiry.

Dined with him and others at the Ton, Billingsgate. At dinner time he was missed; and was found at a fishmonger's, learning the history of pickled salmon.

In December 1794 Windham paid him a visit, and one day after dinner he said, "I have had a terrible morning. I have been cutting down some trees in the home-wood, and I was there last with my son to mark them. This elm, I said to him, must make way for that old oak: here we will open a walk, and there place an Urn to your Uncle's memory." The recollection of it overcame him.

[Mr. Burke's only son, who had succeeded to the representation in Parliament of the borough of Malton, on his father retiring from it in 1794, died very shortly afterwards, in August, 1794. ED., 1859]

He dictates a good deal to an amanuensis, and corrects repeatedly afterwards, often printing and canceling.

Sir Joshua Reynolds, being fond of the old style of gardening, interceded for a clipt hedge at Beaconsfield, which still stands. He loved to see the footsteps of man about a human habitation.

He [Burke] drank tea with Erskine at Hampstead, after he had left Parliament, and not long before his death. "Here," says he, "you are well placed. Here a Reform can do no harm. Whether you plant nettles or roses, is of no importance. The world will not suffer by it."

Thought the Mosaic account [of the creation] most probable – the creation of a man and a woman, full grown. How otherwise could mankind have been reared?

– Charles James Fox –

I am well aware that these scraps of conversation have little to recommend them, but as serving to shew his playfulness, his love of letters and his good nature in unbending himself to a young man. They were read by his Nephew [Lord Holland] with tears in his eyes. – S.R.

Thought Pope's Eloisa to Abelard "about half and half;" and particularly disliked "Give all thou canst," &c.; and "Oh! make me mistress to the man I love," only a common vulgar sentiment, and not as it is in her letters "the wife of Abelard." Eloisa much greater in her letters than Pope had made her.

When Francis said that Wilberforce, if it was left to him to decide whether Pitt should go out of office for ten months and the Slave-trade be abolished for ever, or Pitt remain in – with the Slave-trade, would decide for Pitt – "Yes," said Fox, "I'm afraid he would be for Barabbas."

Mentioned the extreme uneasiness he felt, when he spent even a single day in a town where he did not know the language. "You are imposed upon," says Tierney, "without even the satisfaction of knowing it." "Not only that," says Fox.

He reads all the Novels.

Thought Iphigénia the English for Iphigenía, as Virgil is for Virgilius.

"I should not care," said he, "if I was condemned never to stir beyond a mile from St. Ann's Hill for the rest of my life."

I always say, and always think, that of all the countries in Europe, England will be the last to be free. Russia will be free before England. The Russians know no better, and knowledge might and would operate on them to good; but the English have the knowledge and the slavery too.

A man must have a grand want of right feeling and right thinking, who does not like popularity, who does not wish the people about him, and for and with whom he acts, to be in good humour with him.

I love establishments, and love law; but I detest the priests and the lawyers.

Were I to be tried, I would as soon be at the mercy of the bishops as the judges; though the Archbishop of Armagh said to me twenty-five years ago – "Take care. The bishops would burn you if they could."

The French verse very bad; as every syllable, except where there is a feminine termination, should be pronounced *equally*, which cannot be in the French verse; and therefore it continually tortures the ear.

Thought poetry "the great refreshment of the human mind," the only thing after all; – that not a sum of arithmetic could be cast up at first without the aid of poetry. That men first found out they had minds by making and tasting poetry. That Lauderdale was the only man he ever knew, (he did not mean to pay him a compliment) who thought rightly on many things, without the love of poetry.

Everything is to be found in Homer.

Justified Roscoe's "Nearly two centuries' saw" as a loose way of writing, and not properly a metaphor.

Detested such as Johnson's "Existence saw him spurn her bounded reign" – and not less the second line, "And panting time toiled after him in vain," as not only inelegant, but contrary to our ideas of time, which is generally represented as swift.

[*Drury Lane prologue, 1747:*

> *"When Learning's triumph o'er her barb'rous foes*
> *First rear'd the stage, immortal Shakespeare rose;*
> *Each change of many-colour'd life he drew,*
> *Exhausted worlds, and then imagin'd new:*
> *Existence saw him spurn her bounded reign,*
> *And panting time toil'd after him in vain," &c.*

ED., 1859]

When Courtenay was walking in his garden at St. Ann's, he asked for the kitchen garden; – "You are now in the midst of it," replied Fox; it is intermixed with the shrubs and flowers, and plays its part among them.

Mrs. Armistead, when he returns fretted in an evening, takes down a volume of Don Quixote or Gil Blas, and reads him into tranquillity.

N. Poussin the only Painter who purposely omitted to do what he could. In his landscapes brilliant, in his historical pictures dead – certainly intended them to represent antient ones.

Neither Homer nor Virgil mention the singing of Birds.

[*In a letter to Mr. Rogers, from a much valued friend, the Honorable Edward Everett, lately ambassador from the United States, dated 24 Dec. 1850, the writer points out that Mr. Fox was here in error, as far as Virgil is concerned; and refers to the Æneid, VIII. 456: – "Et matutini volucrum sub culmine cantus."* ED., 1859]

Thought the idea of collecting these fine things from all parts of the world a noble one, and believed it was conceived by Bonaparte. Said it was a delightful walk, but by some impulse of the mind, one always looked at the same pictures. Had not been there for three weeks.

The French had a right to these spoils of a conquered Country.

Looked out of the Gallery Window, and thought the sun was burning up his turnips.

Portraits: – wished he had sat only to Sir Joshua Reynolds. Said his sitting so often for his portrait was owing to her [Mrs. Fox], though he liked Nollekens's last bust, and thought it the best of all the likenesses.

Cupid blind not older than the Italians.

Tired of the ballet.

Mrs. Fox said the only fault she could find with him was his aversion to music. The utmost she could say for him was that he *could* read Homer, while she played and sung to herself.

English the most difficult of all languages – an union of many. Found King William wrote bad French – "Mon toux" instead of "Ma toux." The English articulate very ill. Gibbon, if anybody, mastered two languages.

Milton not English – could never forgive him for expecting to interest him through twelve books, in which there was nothing like nature; or for writing anything but English – full of inversions and affected phrases. Confessed himself an anti-miltonite – acknowledged the beauty of "beat out life," and of his use of little words.

[*See Adam's vision of the sacrifices by Cain and Abel, and the death of Abel:*

"His offering soon propitious fire from Heaven
Consum'd with nimble glance, and grateful
         steam;
The other's not, for his was not sincere;

Whereat he inly rag'd, and, as they talk'd,
Smote him into the midriff with a stone
That beat out life," &c.

Paradise Lost, XI. 444-6. Ed., 1859]

Virgil remarkable for giving every incident a melancholy ending: – Orpheus and Eurydice – Dido – Nisus and Euryalus – Lausus, &c. – A very melancholy man: Homer not so. Virgil wrote beautiful lines – his story has no interest.

Pope's comparison in his preface to Homer. When a man writes a preface, he tries only to say an antithesis, and never thinks of the truth.
[*A comparison of Homer with Virgil runs throughout the preface.* Ed., 1859]

Homer – the interview between Priam and Achilles his finest passage; Priam's kissing the hands of him who had slain his son! Helen's lamentation over Hector. None more mistaken than those who think Homer has no delicacy; he is full of it. Thought nothing more unlike Homer's similes than Milton's. Did Penelope *never* name Troy? He had remarked that delicacy, and also her not mentioning Ulysses by name.

I said in one respect the French had the advantage

of us. He said, indeed in almost every respect.

Observed of Gibbon's History that if a man was to say, "I can't read it," and was to attempt to acquire the knowledge it contained by any other means, he would find it a hard task. Robertson very superficial in comparison.

Thought the music of the antients must have been as superior as their sculpture and poetry.

Thought Virgil's Georgics the most difficult thing to translate in the World: – Milton's Paradise Lost less so. Fitzpatrick mentioned a translator unacquainted with the language of his original, and to whom it was translated by another. Fox said he did not know whether that was not the best way – it would lead to more freedom and less attention to words. Desirous to know which were the three translations considered by Warton as superior to the originals – Hampton's Polybius – Rowe's Lucan – and Melmoth's Pliny. To the French remark that a translator resembled a rope-dancer, he said Pope was an exception. (I suppose he meant as to the risk he ran.)

Said of all pictures which came nearest to perfection in colour, and which united most of the great qualities of the Art, was Titian's St. Peter Martyr.

Petrifactions – many [there in Paris] from Milan. Here he was very animated – could scarcely bring himself to believe what he saw – fish in perfection inclosed in stone! Birds and Beasts – Had seen these before, but brought General Fitzpatrick, who delighted in curious birds – The little birds – Mrs. F. said that she and Mr. F. spent much of their time in watching the motions of the little birds, when building, and rearing their young. Particularly struck with the jealousy of the bullfinch, the most jealous of all birds.

Vote for the King's death. Fox said that all, he believed, who were acted upon by fear, voted for it. They were afraid of the public cry.

Had just read Euripides. Alcestis his favourite. Hercules's resolution, "I must do some great thing. I have used them ill." Heraclides, "And these men wore Greek habits!" – he repeated these instances twice. [*This is a very* free *translation by Mr. Fox . . . Here, again, Mr. Fox gives the effect rather than a translation.* ED., 1859]

The Greek Historians were all true; the Romans liars, particularly Livy, who never scrupled to tell a story as he pleased.

The Queen a bad woman – The King distrustful of everybody – not from education only. There is such a thing as a suspicious nature. The Prince quick; he would not have ventured to treat the Princess as he did publicly, if not encouraged by somebody.

Ministers wish for peace, but have not the courage to be peaceable.

Robertson's life of Columbus *well written*.

Pope's sylphs are the prettiest invention in the world, but will never do again.

Lear, Othello, Macbeth, the best plays of Shakespeare. First act of Hamlet pre-eminent – the ghost the first ever conceived in every respect – Hamlet not really mad. Wonders whether Shakespeare had ever seen a translation of Euripides – so like him in many places – particularly in Queen Catherine's taking leave of her servants, where he reminds you of Alcestis.

Metastasio. He wrote indeed in a most poetical language; but that was not his fault.

Read Homer more than once a year.

A distant prospect indispensable for a house.

Wondered I was not partial to rhyme. The antients could do without it; but their verse was not superior to it. It is at least equal to antient verse, and perhaps the most perfect thing yet invented. It is a thing to repose upon, and often suggests the thought. Blank verse is perhaps best for dramatic poetry.

Vanbrugh almost as great a genius as ever lived. Sir John Brute – "And this woman will get a husband!"

Josephine a very pleasing woman.

He loved children.

The poets wrote the best prose – Cowley's very sweet; Milton's excepted – more extravagant than his verse, as if written in ridicule of the latter.

Who do you think the best writer of our time? I'll tell you who I think – Blackstone.

Very candid – Retracts instantly – Continually putting wood on the fire –

Read aloud one evening in the library Gray's fragment, "Scent the new fragrance of the breathing rose." It was rather unlucky that the rose blew in the north of Europe.

If he had a boy, would make him write verses; the only way of knowing the meaning of words.

Ghosts and witches the best machinery for a modern epic.

Johnson's preface to Shakespeare the best thing on the subject. His treatment of Gray, Waller, and Prior abominable; especially Gray. As for me *I love all the poets.*

Lord Lansdowne certainly a magnificent man; with no remarkable taste for pictures or fine things, but thinking them fit for a man of his station, and wishing at least to acquire distinction in that way.

Lord Bute still more a magnificent man than Lord Lansdowne, with more taste, that is, more love for those things.

Blenheim wanted buildings in the grounds; admired the *private* ride round by the water.

Pope failed most, I think, in sense – he seldom knew what he meant to say.

Romeo and Juliet – In the play Romeo dies before Juliet awakes – not so in the novel, and better, and not now acted so.

Are there any antient fables?

I have no faith in Bruce. To hear him talk is enough.

Pope – Eloisa to Abelard is full of passion and beauty, though many things in it might be wished otherwise.

Congreve rich – wrote little – seldom seen – did not make himself cheap – therefore so highly rated by his contemporaries.

I write with difficulty. Perhaps with the greater ease a man speaks, with the greater difficulty he writes. I believe so.

Pictures – I like them.

Trees – birds – nightingales – No antient and no modern poets except the English mention much the singing of birds. Virgil not once in his Georgics – doubts whether Catullus's Passer was more than a little bird.

Doubtful whether he should introduce notes into his history – had determined against it. Much perplexed how to interweave his new matter from Paris into the text already written. Should he use dashes or not? Wished much to introduce speeches but said it would not do.

[*History of Reign of James II.* ED., 1859]

Lord Hervey's verses on Pope very good, though Burke did not think so.

Pope's letters very bad – I think him a foolish fellow, upon the whole, myself, but he has certainly feeling; and I like him best when not a satirist.

Gray – no man with that face could have been a man of sense. His Essay on Education and his Churchyard, his best works. The Nile! – (when he came to that passage in reading it, his face brightened, his voice rose, and he looked to me) – A very learned and extraordinary man.

> [*"What wonder, in the sultry climes, that spread*
> *Where Nile redundant o'er his summer-bed*
> *From his broad bosom life and verdure flings,*
> *And broods o'er Egypt with his wat'ry wings,*
> *If with advent'rous oar and ready sail*
> *The dusky people drive before the gale."*
>
> *The Alliance of Education.* ED., 1859]

Repeated with Mrs. Fox that song of Mrs. Barbauld's, "Come here, fond youth, who e'er thou be" – the first verse full of bad grammar.

Gibbon a great coxcomb – his portrait by Sir Joshua Reynolds is over the fire-place at Lausanne, and he used to look at it as often as if it had been his mistress's. – Observed again that if any man were to say, "I don't like his history, I will acquire the information another way," he would find it a very hard task.

Temples in gardens – wished for a temple to the Muses – wished any body would let him build him one. Lord Newburgh a man of great taste – has built a temple for *me*; perhaps there are too many at Stowe.

Lansdowne Library – always liked it – so vast, so retired – the antient chimney-piece – always liked the idea of a large room in the midst of a great city – lighted from the sky and into which you could go and say – "I shut you all out." Saw one at Dublin – belonging to Lord Charlemont.

A distance essential to a house.

Nobody but very young girls could like Lovelace – perhaps *they* might.

Always think of what Lord *** used to say, that nothing is so easy as for young people to make fools of old people whenever they please.

Liked to meet with grand houses in wild and desert places – to step from dreariness into splendid apartments. Chatsworth struck him particularly in this way.

All roads from town are disagreeable – the Kensington road is thought the best, but it must be on account of its setting out through Hyde Park.

Sir Joshua Reynolds had no pleasure at Richmond – he used to say the human face was his landscape.

A foolish song "When lovely woman stoops to folly" – a bad rhyme to melancholy.

Raleigh a very fine writer. Lord Surrey too old.

Always thought Mason to blame for suppressing Gray's translations – surely the most valuable kind of thing to an English reader is a good translation.

Sir Joshua Reynolds – the grand not his forte. Liked best his playful characters.

Revival of letters – Where would you begin? with the Medici? then you leave those men behind you. The middle ages never very dark; always producing some able men.

There is nothing more in favour of wine than the many disagreeable substitutes for it which are used in countries where it is not found; such as betel-root, opium, &c.

After all Burke was a damned wrong-headed fellow through life – always jealous and contradictory.

No man, I maintain, could be ill-tempered, who wrote so much nonsense as Swift.

I have no idea of Physiognomy and its rules as to the mind; perhaps right sometimes as to the temper. Lord Redesdale a remarkably silly looking man; and so indeed in reality. Pitt, I cannot see any indications of sense in him – did not you know what he is you would not discover any.

How delightful to lie on the grass, with a book in your hand all day – Yes – but why with a book?

In a letter-writing mood wrote to Dr. Bardsley of Manchester on his pamphlet against Bull-baiting.

Not against it himself; thought the outcry against the common people unjust, while their betters hunted and fished. Was decidedly in favour of boxing.
[*Samuel Argent Bardsley, M.D., on the Use and Abuse of Popular Sports and Exercises.* – Mem. Manch. Soc. *vol. I.?* ED., 1859]

Had written to Roscoe concerning proper names – disapproved altogether of his practice. His instance of Louis, in the introduction, particularly against him.
[*Roscoe, in his preface to his Life of Leo X, published shortly before the date of this conversation, had justified the practice he had adopted of designating the scholars of Italy by their national appellations; and of his spelling the name of the King of France as* Louis XII, *(the name he himself recognized,) and not* Lewis XII, *which latter spelling Roscoe admitted to be the English mode.* Pref. to Leo X. 1st edit. *It appears by Roscoe's later editions that he was not induced by Mr. Fox's criticism to alter his practice.* ED., 1859]

Hume – his quotations at full length from other writers – sometimes altered in the language for no purpose – as in the case of a passage from Burnet, whose language certainly required no alteration. The practice of quoting gave great variety to his style.

Homer – Iliad and Odyssey – Knight was coming to read his arguments why they were written by different people – Was inclined to say he *would* not believe it.

Mrs. Barbauld's life of Richardson admirable – always wished she had written more, and not misspent her time in writing books for children, now multiplied beyond all bounds – though hers were the best.

It was the fashion to say surgeons were always right.

The only foundation for toleration is a degree of skepticism; and without it there can be none. For if a man believes in the saving of souls, he must soon think about the means; and if, by cutting off one generation, he can save many future ones from Hellfire, it is his duty to do it.

Never heard Burke say he was no Christian; but had no reason to think he was one – certainly no papist.
Virgil's "O fortunatos, &c." the most beautiful thing in the world, and with less of his melancholy than usual, which is so apt to break out in every part of him – his "sua si bona" indeed an exception and very melancholy. Such unaffected tenderness in Virgil!

Ghosts – No man, however theoretically an unbeliever, but practically a believer more or less.

Believes he could repeat all Horace's Odes by tomorrow morning with a little recollection.

Remembers saying to the Bishop of Down at Oxford – "Come, let us have no more study – Let us read all the Plays we can find."

Prefers the Traveller to the Deserted Village on the whole. Knew Goldsmith well, but had heard nothing of him before the Traveller – he was amazingly foolish sometimes.

Foote, at the time, was run down as a Writer and an Actor; but was often excellent in both. So happy in some of his parts. At Lord E. Bentinck's table Foote overcame us, though we had resolved to take no notice of him.

Was Garrick of the original [literary] club? Malone could tell us. That is just what Malone is good for. – Laughed heartily.

Laughed at Johnson's saying Lord Chatham would not suffer Lord Camden to sit down in his presence.

Burke used to say it might be true in part. Laughed again.

Herodotus uses us ill in saying he knows more than he will tell us. Then why say so? Laughed. – A charming writer.

Pork is excellent in all its shapes; and I cannot conceive why it was ever prohibited – it is good in Otaheite, and of course in the East.

The Chinese an odd people. Political Economy is certainly best understood in China.

Virgil soothing – I said I loved sedatives. He said, I don't know – agitations have always been considered as the greatest pleasures.

Sheridan was now all despondence – always in an extreme. Sheridan when talking of his own superiority, often said that he expected wings to shoot out from his elbows.

Gorcum a town in Holland, where nothing was talked but Dutch, and where signs were necessary. Could not remember the name at dinner – Many minutes afterwards stretched his arm across the table, and cried out "Gorcum!" How odd it is to be sure, when one is hunting after a word, when you burn, and think you almost touch him, but not quite – if I had not caught him then, I had lost him.

Often in speaking, when a thing occurs to me and it is not the time to bring it out, I know I shall lose it when I want it, and never fail to do so.

Grattan: his success in our House. Had heard him in Ireland and was confident. Grattan himself was apprehensive. Never was anything so soon decided – in five minutes – though his friends feared, and his enemies were sure of his failure.

Liked wood-strawberries best.

The Bowling-green at Holland-house mown every day – The lawn twice a week – Liked a bowling-green, and lamented he could not make one here.

Should make more garden still, if he could afford it. Liked a garden. Roses so much per pound. Let us plant roses in the wheat-field, if they will fetch so much per pound.

At Lord Keppel's every body so glad to see him so well – could not conceive why, till he found he had been said in the papers to be dangerously ill.

A Bat's wing very beautiful.

"'Tis folly to be *wise*." – 'Tis a misfortune to be knowing, it should be.
[*Gray's Ode on a Distant Prospect of Eton College.* ED., 1859]

Every farmer stops his horse in the lane, and talks with him over the pales about the corn and the weather.

Fitzpatrick not quite so severe a critic as he seems – he makes a face and turns up his brow.

Hippocrates. Thought all the extracts from him admirable, and determined to read him – had never possessed him – admired particularly his Aphorism, "The second best remedy is better than the best, if the patient likes it best."

Could not bear the sight of honey-dew.

Could not remember a line of his own speeches.

Nobody dies! What becomes of all the people? Inimitable acting of — in saying this.

Lord Nugent – clever! You would not have thought him so, had you known him. Old "Remote from Liberty and Truth," as Burke used to call him.
[*A short ode by Lord Nugent "to William Pulteney Esq." commences with the words "Remote from Liberty and Truth".* ED., 1859]

"It is our opinion," &c. in the Morning Chronicle – Laughed heartily – Nothing diverts me more than their opinion – the tone of the Papers!

Duke of Northumberland, visited by a tiger, when in the gout at Northumberland house – have heard him tell the story.

Proposed to go on Saturday – Not before Monday at least – We shall have company to-morrow – let us have a quiet day before we part.

Plutarch – one circumstance prevents my taking any pleasure in his lives – my disbelief of every thing he says – Plutarch's credulity incredible.

Juvenal a *good* writer. Wish he was less difficult.

Gibbon's account of Christianity in his History full of admirable irony.

Dryden's defence of transubstantiation the best passage in perhaps the first poem [*The Hind and the Panther*] in the world. One good trait in him; never but once insolent to fallen greatness.

Cannot read Black Letter – could never make anything of an act of Parliament.

Johnson felt little respect for short poems.

Boswell I believe to be full of veracity.

Did any body in our time remember Johnson in early life before his celebrity? How did he behave then?

Sir William Jones drew from a very ample fund.

I do not like geese upon a Common; they make a bad soil; nor do I like a Common too near me.

Was a famous trap-ball player – beat some Etonians two or three years ago.

Bonaparte a spoiled child. Berthier, who was much with him, said that when out rabbit shooting, if he missed, and they hit, he did not like it, and grew very cross.

Czar Peter's dreadful punishment of drawing under the keel.

Water and all White Wines improved by ice.

Sir Charles Grandison an Eneas-kind of character.

Bond Street bad, and inferior to what the Strand used to be, which has suffered in its shops from Bond Street – Piccadilly on a bright Sunday very fine. Could never believe the streets of London were so short as they are – particularly Bond Street, which is said to be only half a mile long.

Thought Gibbon's acacia-walk long; and it was short.
[*The acacia walk in Gibbon's garden at Lausanne, so touchingly connected with his reflections on the completion of his history of the Decline and Fall.* ED., 1859]

Never liked Ranelagh, though one should not, they say, speak ill of the dead.
[*Ranelagh was discontinued in 1802.* ED., 1859]

Alliteration; I believe it is peculiar to the English, if we except that ridiculous one of Cicero.

Preferred the Spanish Proverb to any – "The biter bit" – how inferior to "He went out to gather wool, and comes home shorn" – quoting the Spanish.

That a man is young at forty I always maintain.

Voltaire's works. I often look at them on the shelf, and wonder they are really an object for contemplation! Voltaire repeats himself very often of course, or it could not be.

When he said he carved ill, and she confirmed it – "Yes, my dear, I thought you would agree with me."

Speaking of the new room projecting – "Then you'll be always in the new drawing-room – you'll never play again where I am – never more in the poor back room."

Homer almost always speaks well of women, except in the instance of Penelope's maids, whom he uses rather hardly.

Read nine Epic Poems aloud to Mrs. Fox, in one winter, (if I could call Lucretius one, which it is not;) Iliad, Odyssey, Apollonius Rhodius, Eneid, Tasso, Ariosto, Milton's Paradise Lost, and Regained, Fairy Queen. Two of them far the most entertaining to read, whatever may be their other merits – The Odyssey, and The Orlando Furioso.

Like a book of Spenser exceedingly, before something else.

Have often thought that if I had a great deal of leisure, I would publish an edition of Dryden – with the originals on the opposite page to the Translations.

Nothing so absurd as not to give Chaucer with the Translations.

Broke from a Criticism on Porson's Euripides, to look for the little pigs.

Garrick's Othello reminded Quin of a little black boy with a tea-kettle; and I always looked for the tea-kettle.

Darwin recommended cold bathing for a cold – Coke the worse for it – try again, said Darwin.

When Mackintosh reflected on O'Quigley what was the reply of Parr? "He was an Irishman, and he might have been a Scotchman – He was a Priest, and he might have been a Lawyer – He was a Rebel, and he might have been an Apostate."

Wasn't it enough to make one cry when the air was so thick last week?

It is always said, Spend your money while you can enjoy it – Now, I always thought money of most use in old age, and it is rather hard upon me that I should want it now.

I can excuse almost everything in Elizabeth but the execution of Mary – Except William the third she was the best of them – We have not had a good set.

William had great simplicity of character; and what is remarkable, the more you know of him the more you like him – his letters are a proof of this. He did nothing perhaps to blame, but in the affair of the massacre of Glencoe; and then not in the thing it-self, for he knew nothing of it, but in pushing too far the maxim, to protect those who only exceed your orders.

I often think that if Elizabeth had invited Philip the second, and had got him over here and clapped him into prison on some pretence of treason or some such thing, it would have saved her a great deal of trouble.

The Odes to Spring and to Adversity his favourites – the first perhaps without faults – but after all, he liked best the Elegy, which is full of faults – the first stanza very bad, "to darkness and to me."

Nothing like the former fashion of high carriages to suit only the young and the active who least wanted to get into them.

Lord Strafford's speech on his trial capital.

No dark ages – Hildebrand's as dark as any, yet his *writing* is good.

Eloisa's letters, what good latin!

Whenever I hated chess, it was like a lover.

Euripides perhaps the most precious thing left us – most like Shakespeare.

Cæsar's Commentaries do not entertain me somehow. There is a want of thought in them – dry, and affecting to be written briefly and in a hurry – Came here; went there.

All serves to convince me that women must have a great influence in Society, do what you will.

Bonaparte very handsome, and more like Lord

Villiers than any body in England – though certainly not so handsome. The smiles that played about his mouth when he spoke delightful.

Have not seen the hills this fortnight. When in the evening it suddenly cleared – "How d'ye do?" he cried, laughing.

Thought of his game of chess in the night. Does not play slow, but talks and reasons a good deal while playing. Played eight games with me and won five.

Said to himself, on one occasion, that he was sure he was wrong, he had been so positive.

When I said, speaking of the East wind, I wish the new Administration would get it put down by Act of Parliament, he smiled, and said, (waking as it were, out of one of his fits of torpor) "They would find *that* a difficult thing – but I believe they would do as much good in that, as they will in anything else." – *Lord Holland.*

When a bitter wind in March blew from the West; and after a time the weathercock shifted to the East – "Yes," he would say, laughing, "I knew it would own itself East at last." – *Lord Holland.*

I am, as he said of himself, a very pains-taking man. When he first entered into office, being dissatisfied with his hand-writing he took lessons; and for some time, when carving, he had a book on the subject open by him. – *Lord Holland.*

If I recover, Young one, I will never take an efficient office again; though I should like to be useful. I will never be so foolish as to take a peerage; a thing I have often refused. – *Lord Holland.*

My Uncle was humorous on sad occasions. When helping him into bed a night or two before he died, I said, "O passi graviora: dabit Deus his quoque finem" – he replied, "Aye, young one – but *finem* is an awkward word in more senses than one." – *Lord Holland.*

– Henry Grattan –

Strafford an unprincipled man, flattering his master to his ruin; with no talent but eloquence, I rejoice in his fall when I read of it.

It was right that Charles should die; he had made war on his people; but the thing was ill done. He was put to death by a party, and not by a power emanating from the people.

Old men love society. Hope is the food of solitude; and young men like to be alone.

Historians are not contented with telling us what was done, but they pretend to enter into the secret motives of men.

Pitt could not have much knowledge. His father had but little. Burke used to say of Lord Chatham, "His forte was fancy, and his feeble was ignorance." Pitt has ruined his country.

Like Louis XIV, he returns the bow of a child.

Reasoned on the creation and government of the world. (It is a singular inference to make that because this world is imperfect, he who made it has made better.)

Swift was on the wrong side in England; but in Ireland he was a Giant.

Gulliver's Travels amusing; but is there much to be learned from them?

Were you twenty years old, and Captain Cook setting sail, would you go round the world with him? No, I have no wish to see such countries as he saw. I wish to see Rome and Athens, and some parts of Asia; but little besides.

Was shut up when a boy to read Plutarch's lives, and could not bear the confinement – used to read five pages, and doze away the rest of the time. Thinks now, however, that Brutus's life is very affecting towards the end.

Would sooner be shot than ascend in a balloon.

One of the reasons why the affairs of Nations are not better conducted, is that the consequences of our misconduct are more remote, and less certain, than any false step we may make in private life. A nation may be ruined, but not in our time; nor will the causes that led to it be so obvious as to attach certainty to such or such a person. We may not live to see the tragedy, nor indeed may it ever take place. Our self-interest, in that respect, is therefore less awake, and so also are our consciences; nor is our imagination so excited by the prospect of evil to many as to one. Our self-interest, as individuals, which is generally short-sighted, counteracts the other too powerfully.

Were I rich, and could I live as I please, I should have no wish for a fine house or fine furniture, (I would rather not have them, I should be afraid of hurting them) or pictures – they give me no pleasure. I would have no fine gardens or conservatories – I love the fruit; but I would have no fine gardener to criticize me, and tell me I was doing wrong, or walking awkwardly – I should love a wide expanse – I would have bands of music – I love music – I would have a carriage for use, and fine horses, but not for riding – I love to go fast – I would cut the air.

Wealth makes a man sad – he lives for others who don't care for him; – he becomes a steward.

My Uncle Dean Marlay was famous for the best little dinners, and the best company in Dublin – but when made a Bishop he enlarged his table, and he lost his fame – he had no more good company – and there was an end of his enjoyment. He had at first about four hundred pounds a year, and his dinners were delightful; but he had an estate left him, and afterwards came to a Bishoprick – he had Lords and Ladies to his table – people of fashion – foolish men and foolish women, and there was an end of him and of us.

I cannot bear large and mixed companies; they make me miserable.
[*Mrs. G. complains that he ought to bear his share in them; but he won't; he has no voice for them. S.R.*]

A fine prospect to the visitor or traveller is ever delightful – but possession destroys the pleasure. If I delighted much in a view or a spot, I would wish some other person to live there.

What is a Ghost? A dead man alive? If immaterial, it can be no object of sight.

Were a man to be offered life, with a foresight of all the evils that attend it, would he not reject it?

Pitt's faults might arise in some degree from his situation. For twenty years he was an apologist for failure, and an imposer of taxes: in other words a humbug.

Standing under the Limes – "Now what are these senators about? A great bumble-bee is now addressing them – they are now in a Committee." It was June, and the Limes were full of bees. He used to say in a morning, "Shall we visit those senators?"

Burke's speeches far better to read than to hear. They are better suited to a patient reader, than to an impatient hearer.

A woman in a red cloak passed us with her chattels on her back – "That woman is to be envied. She has nothing to lose, and everything to gain – She has therefore hope – no thoughts of invasion – none of taxes."

He seems not to have admired Fox's speaking towards the last; thinking that he fell off as his infirmities gained ground upon him.

Poetry transfused into prose, no plagiarism – difficult to give it a prose flow, and to melt it into the sentence.

Raphael and Adam; their interview in Paradise Lost a model of high breeding.

Liked Spa, where all the great people in Europe met in dishabille.

Which would you rather pass a day with, Alexander, Cæsar, or Bonaparte? Cæsar, as I am much interested about his time. I would ask him, (and here he enumerated many questions about his campaigns) what were the real characters of many of his contemporaries – and I would ask him, but I would not press the question, (he might answer it or not as he pleased) what part he took in the Catiline conspiracy.

In travelling, I should like the lower orders of the people better than the middle ones, for my companions – I would rather be in a heavy coach than in one that carried four.

Of all men, if I could call up one, it should be Scipio Africanus. Hannibal was perhaps a greater Captain, but not so great and good a man. Epaminondas did not do so much. Themistocles was a rogue.

Modern times have not furnished such men. It required the competition in little states.

In modern times Washington, I believe, was the greatest man, and next to him, William the Third.

Decorated himself with Lime-blossoms, and stood again under the Lime-trees. Found a winged ant carrying a caterpillar.

Would you wish to call up Cleopatra? Not much – her beauty would make me sad, and she would tell me nothing but lies.

Priam very well-bred, particularly towards Helen.

Hume right in saying, that not a page in Shakespeare was without glaring faults. In Othello he seems to have indulged in an Eastern style of speaking.

Sheridan's faults, like those of most men of genius; which are almost all of a poetical character – the excesses of the generous virtues.

What a slavery is office – to be subject to the whims of those above you, and the persecutions of those beneath you – to dance attendance on the great – to be no longer your own master. – No, give me a cottage and a crust – plain fare and quiet, and small beer, and, he added, lowering his voice and smiling with his usual archness, "Claret."

Mrs. Anne Pitt, Lord Chatham's sister, a very superior woman – She hated him, and they lived like dog and cat. She said he had never read but one book – The Faery Queen. He could only get rid of her by leaving his house, and setting a bill upon it, "This house to let."

Every sentence [of Fox] came rolling like a wave of the Atlantic, three thousand miles long.

Burke was so fond of arbitrary power, he could not sleep upon his pillow, unless he thought the King had a right to take it from under him.

Lord Chatham made his son read to him, a day or two before he died, the conclusion of Pope's Homer, describing the death of Hector; and when he had done he said, "Read it again."

Stella used often to visit my aunt, and sleep with her in the same bed, and weep all night. She was not very handsome. Miss V— *was* handsome.
[*Mrs. Johnson, whom Swift has celebrated under the name of Stella; and to whom he was privately married. Miss Vanhomrigh, whom Swift called Vanessa.*
Ed., 1859]

There is now a state religion – not a Christian religion.

Beauty is the best thing going. To Beauty we owe Poetry, to Poetry Civilization, to Civilization every art and science.

Two artists have contributed not a little to the popularity of Charles the First, Vandyke and the Headsman.

Milton I like best of them all. He is much more poetical than Shakespeare; and if anybody would be a public speaker, let him study his prose and his poetry – his prose is often an admirable model for the majestic style of speaking.

To be a good shot is useful. It makes a brave man braver, a timid man half-brave; and all men are born cowards. But it makes a bad man worse than it found him – a bully.

Who was the best speaker you ever heard? Fox, during the American War – Fox in his best days; about the year 1779.

Using the word Disloyalty in the sense it has been used in, makes the King the Law.

Lord Chatham. "I don't enquire from what quarter the wind cometh, but whither it goeth; and if any measure that comes from the Right Honorable Gentleman tends to the Public Good, my bark is ready." – "I stand alone – I stand like our first ancestor – naked, but not ashamed."

Lord Chatham, I think, delivered finer things than Demosthenes; but he had a greater theatre, and men are made by circumstances. "America has resisted. I rejoice, my Lords." This passage, I think, excels any in Demosthenes.
[*The speech was not in the Lords, but in the Commons, on 14th Jan. 1766.* ED., 1859]

Castle-building is a bad habit. It leads to disappointment.

Solitude is bad. I have tried Tinnehinch for twenty-years – It leads to melancholy – to a sort of madness – You think of your vexations, your age. – Society should always be in your power.
[*Mr. Grattan's residence in the county of Wicklow.* ED., 1859]

An old man cannot enjoy solitude. He has learnt the secret – He has found out the rogueries of Fortune. Nor will reading supply the want. I would live in a house full of society, to which I might escape from myself.

I was called the Spirit of the Dargle. I found out (he said, laughing) that a man's worst companion is himself.
[*A glen, near Tinnehinch.* ED., 1859]

The King (Charles the First) had made war on the people – but the death of Strafford was less to be justified – Though a thief, a robber, he was no traitor. He had committed every crime but that for which he was condemned to die.

Of what use is it? (Lycidas), says Johnson. These things – they take the mind out of the dirt, as it were.

The French poets I read with little pleasure; and am glad when I have done. Boileau perhaps – but such is their homage to the great, we are the worse for them.

A wife should be of a modest character. She should sing.

We should always have the appearance of narrative, not of description.

Dislikes the clergy and all humbugs.

[*His forte in conversation is sketching a character, with a gentle voice and many pauses; but with a*

delicate irony, a great archness of look and manner;
beginning, as you would think, with something like
praise, and ending with a roll of the person and a turn
of the head, in a coup de Patte. It is very delightful
to see him with Miss Fox. The enjoyment she feels
encourages him. S.R.]

Pitt would be right nineteen times for once that Fox
would be right: but that once would be worth all the
rest. The heart is wiser than the schools.

In conversation, said Plunket, he gave results rather
than processes of reasoning. Every sentence was a
treasure.
[*As I can say of all the eminent men I have known,*
and from them, generally speaking, I have learnt more
than from books, what they said making a deeper im-
pression. S.R.]

When Dr. Lucas, a very unpopular man, ventured
on a speech in the Irish Parliament, and failed altogether, Grattan said, "He rose without a friend, and
sat down without an enemy."

Of — he said: "He was a coward in the field, and
a bully in the street."

– Lord Grenville –

M r. Fox's speeches were full of repetition. He used to say that it was necessary to hammer it into them; but I rather think he could not do otherwise.

Nothing more shows the malice of some of Milton's biographers, than the pleasure they take in relating that Milton suffered corporal punishment at college. It was then and long afterwards in constant use at both Universities; nor would it have been anything unusual, if he had received it; but it is no where said that he had. The lines quoted from him by Johnson are followed by others from which it may be clearly inferred that he suffered rustication, and therefore not corporal punishment. A good life of Milton is much wanted. No man ever acted up to his belief of what was right, more conscientiously and firmly.

Lord Chatham, according to Mrs. A. Pitt, was always

reading Spenser. "He who knows Spenser," says Burke, "has a good hold on the English tongue." [*Mrs. Anne Pitt told Mr. Grattan that Lord Chatham has never read but one book – The Faery Queene.* ED., 1859]

Gibbon's notes are delightful.

Earl St. Vincent a great man. He enforced discipline at the expence of his popularity. Not rewarded as he deserved; but the late King had many prejudices: he was perhaps the narrowest mind I ever knew.

Locke an extraordinary man, though in metaphysics he blundered about ideas, and though in politics he believed in an original compact; (how can a man bind his grandchild unborn?) In theology I am told, by those who understand those matters, that he erred most of all.

He sits, summer and winter, on the same sofa, his favourite books on the shelves just over his head.

Roger Ascham's style laboured and artificial. Yet I often read him. Here he is just above me.

Milton always within reach.

We sat down to rest in the Pinery seat, inscribed
 "Pulcherrima pinus in hortis,"
and the clock of the stables struck twelve. Few
things, he said, affect me more than a clock – its
duration – its perseverance – the same voice, morning, noon, and night. There is somewhere a good account of a castle-clock in the Mysteries of Udolpho.
"That old fellow crowed through the siege, and is
crowing still." Yes, says he (the clock was then striking) that voice will be heard long after I am in my
grave and forgotten. [*Not forgotten, S.R.*]

You have not named the best style in its way: –
Blackstone's.

Raleigh's "O eloquent, just, and mighty Death,"
one of the finest, if not the finest, passage in English
prose.

Castlereagh ignorant to the last, with no princi-
ple or feeling, right or wrong. Before he spoke, he
would collect what he could on the subject, but
never spoke above the level of a newspaper. Had
three things in his favour, tact, good humour, and
courage.

Never was such a thing done, as sending a cabinet
minister to Vienna to act as he pleased, one who was

irresponsible, one who knew nothing, and who had never looked into a map.

Gibbon's best work, his review of the Roman Empire in the first volume, his only instance of generalizing.

In his earlier life he [Pitt] was gay and delightful in conversation. At last his temper clouded. Dr. Addington ruined his health. Port wine was Addington's great remedy; and at Hayes I used to wonder at the bumpers they were drinking, confined as I was to water. Afterwards it became necessary to him; and though never more affected by it than others in general, he certainly drank freely.

He was fond of Holwood, and showed taste in the planting; but he mismanaged the water sadly; and laughed when I remonstrated against his leveling, as he did, part of the fortification in the Roman camp there. All the Roman remains among us, and whatever related to Gothic or ancient times, he held in no great respect.

[*Holwood, near Bromley, in Kent; Mr. Pitt's residence.* Ed., 1859]

I once sent a short-hand writer to take notes of his [Pitt's] speeches; but the notes were so imperfect that the scheme failed. All the reporters were against us; and their misrepresentations were with us a constant source of complaint.

I had no great respect for Pope, but was sorry for the destruction of his garden. There was an old summer-house of Burke's at Beaconsfield pulled down; and I have often regretted that I did not buy it and set it up somewhere at Dropmore.
[*At his villa at Twickenham.* Ed., 1859]

What a crime did Lord Verulam commit! I have often looked at him in the House of Lords as he sat there in his insignificance, and have said to myself, "That is the man who pulled down Bacon's House."
[*Gorhambury House, near St. Albans, and within the bounds of Old Verulam. A few ruins of the mansion remained when Mr. Basil Montagu visited the spot in 1829.* Ed., 1859]

– Richard Porson –

Had I a carriage, and did I see a well-dressed person on the road, I would always invite him in, and learn of him what I could.

Lewis 14th was the son of Anne of Austria by Cardinal Richclieu. The man in the mask was Anne's eldest son – I have no doubt of it.

Thanked Heaven he could at any time go without a meal cheerfully – breakfast, dinner, or supper.

Two parties must consent to the publication of a book, the Public as well as the Author.

Mr. Pitt conceives his sentences before he utters them. Mr. Fox throws himself into the middle of his, and leaves it to God Almighty to get him out again.

When Prometheus made man, he had used up all

the water in making other animals; so he mingled his clay with tears.

Porson would almost cry when he spoke of Euripides. "Why should I write from myself, while anything remains to be done to such a writer as Euripides?"

When repeating a generous action from antiquity, or describing a death like Phocion's, his eyes would fill and his voice falter.

All wit true reasoning.

History of the Grand Hum in a 100 Volumes folio. [Hum *as short for* humbug,*"an imposition or hoax" (OED), from 1751, with Garrick in 1753 ("'Twas all a hum"), Coleridge in 1799 ("The Bristol Library is a hum"),* Blackwood's *in 1841 ("Is Homer a hum and the Iliad a hoax?"), and* Punch *in 1885 ("Political honesty's all a big hum"). The Catholic Church, or the Church, or Christianity?* ED., 2011]

I love an octavo; the pages are soon read – the milestones occur frequently.

If I had £3000 Per Ann.: I would have a person constantly dressed, night and day, with fire and candle to attend upon me. (He is an uncertain sleeper.)

I had lived long before I discovered that Wit was Truth.

A conqueror at the Olympic Games applied to Pindar for an Ode – The poet required twenty guineas. – "I could buy a statue for the sum." "Then buy a statue." Again he applied and consented to the Poet's terms. The Ode begins thus: – Unlike a statue, which remains fixed for ever to its pedestal, this Ode shall fly over Greece, every bark on the Egean Sea, every carriage along its shores, shall transport it.

Did he catch this mania of Burney? No, he has it in the natural way, I believe.

I must confess to have a very strong prejudice against all German original Literature.

In drawing a villain we should always furnish him with something that may seem to justify himself to himself.

Like Simonides, I carry all I have about me, pretty nearly.
[See the story in Phaedrus, Lib. iv. Fab. 21, entitled Naufragium Simonidis. The poet was shipwrecked, and to his anxious fellow passengers, who enquired of him why he did not endeavour to save some of his goods,

he replied, "Mecum mea sunt cuncta." Ed., 1859]

Electricity, Electrum; the quality of Amber; because Amber attracts substances.

Virgil has everywhere arranged his words naturally and properly as in prose. No violent transpositions, or inversions; every word is precisely where it ought to be.

Authority should serve to excite attention, and no farther.

Wit is in general the finest sense in the World.

We all speak in metaphors. Those who appear not to do it, only use those which are worn out, and are overlooked as metaphors. The original fellow is therefore regarded as only witty; and the dull are consulted as the wise.

He has subsisted for three weeks upon a guinea.

Sometimes, at a later period, when he was able enough to pay for a dinner, he chose, in a fit of abstinence, to go without one. I have asked him to stay and dine with me; and he has replied, "Thank you, no; I dined yesterday."

Tooke used to say that "Porson would drink ink rather than not drink at all." Indeed, he would drink any thing. He was sitting with a gentleman, after dinner, in the chambers of a mutual friend, a Templar, who was then ill and confined to bed. A servant came into the room, sent thither by his master for a bottle of embrocation which was on the chimney-piece. "I drank it an hour ago," said Porson.

Next day, Hoppner, somewhat out of temper, informed his wife that Porson had drunk every drop of her concealed dram. "Drunk every drop of it!" cried she: "my God, it was spirits-of-wine for the lamp!"

He would not scruple to return to the dining-room after the company had left it, pour into a tumbler the drops remaining in the wine-glasses, and drink off the omnium gatherum.

At the house of the same gentleman I introduced Cogan to Porson, saying, "This is Mr. Cogan, who is passionately fond of what you have devoted yourself to, – Greek." Porson replied, "If Mr. Cogan is passionately fond of Greek, he must be content to dine on bread and cheese for the remainder of his life."

Porson was fond of smoking, and said that when smoking began to go out of fashion, learning began to go out of fashion also.

One forenoon I met Porson in Covent Garden, dressed in a pea-green coat: he had been married that morning, as I afterward learned from Raine, for he himself said nothing about it.

"I was occupied two years," said Porson, "in composing the *Letters to Travis:* I received thirty pounds for them from Egerton; and I am glad to find that he lost sixteen by the publication."

He thought the *Decline and Fall* beyond all comparison the greatest literary production of the eighteenth century, and was in the habit of repeating long passages from it. Yet I have heard him say that "there could not be a better exercise for a schoolboy than to turn a page of it into *English.*"

When the *Letters to Travis* first appeared, Rennell said to me, "It is just such a book as the devil would write, if he could hold a pen."

When Porson (who had never before seen him) came into the room, he seated himself in an armchair, and looking very hard at Paley, said, "I am entitled to this chair, being president of a society for the discovery of truth, of which I happen at present to be the only member." These words were leveled at certain *political* opinions broached in Paley's works.

He used frequently to regret that he had not gone to America in his youth and settled there. I said, "What would you have done without books?" He answered, "I should have done without them."

At one time he had some thoughts of taking orders, and studied divinity for a year or two. "But," said he, "I found that I should require *about fifty years' reading* to make myself thoroughly acquainted with it, – to satisfy my mind on all points; and therefore I gave it up. There are fellows who go into a pulpit, assuming every thing, and knowing nothing: but *I* would not do so."

He said that every man ought to marry *once*. I observed that every man could not afford to maintain a family. "Oh," replied he, "pap is cheap."

When, however, he went to stay with a friend for only a couple of days or so, he did not encumber himself with a portmanteau: he would merely take a shirt in his pocket, saying, "*Omnia mea mecum porto.*"

The time he wasted in writing notes on the margins of books, – I mean, in writing them with such beauty of penmanship that they rivalled print, – was truly lamentable. And yet he used those very books most cruelly, whether they were his own, or belonging to others: he would let them lie about his room, covered with dust and all sorts of dirt. – He said that "he possessed more *bad* copies of *good* books than any private gentleman in England."

When he was first elected Greek professor, he assured me that he intended to give public lectures in that capacity. I afterwards asked him why he had not given them. He replied, "Because I have thought better on it: whatever originality my lectures might have had, people would have cried out, *We knew all this before.*"

"Indeed, I should like to publish a volume of the curious things which I have gathered in the course of my studies; but people would only say of it, *We knew all this before.*"

Porson, who shrunk on all occasions from praise of himself, was only annoyed by the eulogies which Parr lavished upon him in print. When Parr published the *Remarks on Combe's Statement*, in which Porson is termed "a giant in literature," &c., Porson said, "How should Dr. Parr be able to take the measure of a giant?"

Parr hated Dr. Horsley to such a degree that he never mentioned him by any other name than *the fiend*. – Parr once said to Barker, "You have read a great deal, you have thought very little, and you know nothing."

Burney was indebted to Porson for many of those remarks on various niceties of Greek which he has given as his own in different publications. Porson once said to me, "A certain gentleman" (evidently meaning Burney) "has just been with me; and he brought me a long string of questions, every one of which I answered off-hand. Really, before people become schoolmasters, they ought to get up their Greek thoroughly, for they never learn any thing more of it afterwards." – I one day asked Burney for his opinion of Porson as a scholar. Burney replied, "I think my friend Dick's acquaintance with the Greek dramatists quite marvelous; but he was just as well acquainted with them at the age of thirty as he is now: he has not improved in Greek since he added brandy-and-water to his potations, and took to novel-reading." Porson would sometimes read nothing but novels for a fortnight together.

Now, Porson told Burney expressly, that out of pure kindness he had forborne to mention Wakefield; for he could not have cited any of his emendations without the severest censure.

When Porson was told that Pretyman had been left a large estate by a person who had seen him only once, he said, "It would not have happened, if the person had seen him twice."

When Porson first met Perry after the fire in the house of the latter at Merton, he immediately inquired "if any lives had been lost?" Perry replied "No." "Well," said Porson, "then I shall not complain, though I have lost the labours of my life."

Porson, having good reason to believe that Mathias was the author of the *Pursuits of Literature*, used always to call him "the Pursuer of Literature."

A gentleman who had heard that Bentley was born in the north, said to Porson, "Wasn't he a Scotchman?" – "No, sir," replied Porson; "Bentley was a great Greek scholar."

He said, "Pearson would have been a first-rate critic in Greek, if he had not muddled his brains with divinity."

Porson, of course, did not value the Latin writers so much as the Greek; but still he used to read many of the former with great care, particularly Cicero, of whose *Tusculan Disputations* he was very fond.

For all modern Greek and Latin poetry he had the profoundest contempt. When Herbert published the *Musæ Etonenses*, Porson said, after looking over one of the volumes, "Here is trash, fit only to be put behind the fire."

He dabbled a good deal in Galen.

He cared less about Lucian than, considering the subjects of that writer, you might suppose; the fact was, he did not relish such late Greek.

He read a vast number of French works, and used to say, "If I had a son, I should endeavour to make him familiar with French and English authors, rather than with the classics. Greek and Latin are only luxuries."

He delighted in Milton. "If I live," he exclaimed, "I will write an essay to show the world how unjustly Milton has been treated by Johnson."

A very old gentleman, who had known Johnson

intimately, assured me that the bent of his mind was decidedly towards skepticism; that he was literally afraid to examine his own thoughts on religious matters; and that hence partly arose his hatred of Hume and other such writers.

Porson was passionately fond of Swift's *Tale of a Tub*, and whenever he saw a copy of it on a stall, he would purchase it. He could repeat by heart a quantity of Swift's verses.

Porson would often carry in his pocket a volume of *A Cordial for Low Spirits*.
[*As the* Cordial for Low Spirits, *in three volumes, is now little read, I may mention that it is a very curious collection of controversial pieces, &c., some of which were written by Thomas Gordon (author of* The Independent Whig*), who edited the work. Its heterodoxy did not render it the less acceptable to Porson.* ED., 1859]

On returning from a visit to the Lakes, I told Porson that Southey had said to me, "My *Madoc* has brought me in a mere trifle; but that poem will be a valuable possession to my family." Porson answered, "*Madoc* will be read, – when Homer and Virgil are forgotten" (a *bon-mot* which reached Lord Byron, and which his lordship spoilt).

["*Joan of Arc was marvelous enough; but Thalaba was one of those poems 'which,' in the words of Porson, 'will be read when Homer and Virgil are forgotten,'* – *but* – not till then." *Note on* English Bards and Scotch Reviewers. ED., 1859]

He disliked reading folios, "because," said he, "we meet with so few mile-stones" (*i.e.* we have such long intervals between the turning over of the leaves).

When asked why he had written so little, Porson replied, "I doubt if I could produce any original work which would command the attention of posterity. I can be known only by my notes: and I am quite satisfied if, three hundred years hence, it shall be said that 'one Porson lived towards the close of the eighteenth century, who did a good deal for the text of Euripides.'"

When any one said to him, "Why don't you speak out more plainly on matters of religion?" he would answer, "No, no; I shall take care not to give my enemies a hold upon me."

A man of such habits as Porson was little fitted for the office of Librarian to the London Institution. He never troubled himself about the purchase of books which ought to have been added to the library; and he would frequently come home dead-drunk long after midnight. I have good reason to believe that, had he lived, he would have been requested to give up the office, – in other words, he would have been dismissed. I once read a letter which he received from the Directors of the Institution, and which contained, among other severe things, this cutting remark, – "We only know that you are our Librarian by seeing your name attached to the receipts for your salary." His intimate friend, Dr. Raine, was one of those who signed that letter; and Raine, speaking of it to me, said, "Porson well deserved it." As Librarian to the Institution, he had 200*l*. a-year, apartments rent-free, and the use of a servant. Yet he was eternally railing at the Directors, calling them "mercantile and mean beyond merchandize and meanness."

During the two last years of his life I could perceive that he was not a little shaken; and it is really wonderful, when we consider his drinking, and his total disregard of hours, that he lived so long as he did. He told me that he had had an affection of the lungs from his boyhood.

– Talleyrand –

T hat dispatch which Bonaparte published on his retreat from Moscow, was it written by Himself? By Himself certainly.

Did he shave himself? Always; though he was long about it, shaving a little and then conversing, if any body was with him. A king by birth, said he smiling, is shaved by another. He who makes himself *Roi* shaves himself.

He [Bonaparte] was with the army of England at Boulogne, when he heard of Mack's being at Ulm. "If it had been mine to place him, I should have placed him there." In an instant the army was in full march, and he in Paris. I attended him to Strasburg, and was alone with him in the house of the Prefet – in one of the chambers there – when he fell, and foamed at the mouth. "Fermez la porte," he cried, and from that moment lay as dead on the floor. Berthier came to the door. "On ne peut pas entrer."

The Empress came to the door. "On ne peut pas entrer." In about half an hour he recovered; but what would have been my situation if he had died? Before day-break he was in his carriage, and in less than sixty hours, the Austrian Army had capitulated.

They lived together. Were they married? Pas tout à fait.

Of Lady F— S—'s dress: Il commence trop tard, et finit trop tôt. Comme vous voyez.

Of Robert Smith: C'était donc votre père qui n' était pas si bien.
[*On his praising the beauty of his Mother.* ED., 1859]

Vous savez nager, je crois.
[*In answer to a lady who asked, if she and another lady were both in danger of drowning, which he would help first.* ED., 1859]

I have committed one mistake in life. Et quand finira t'elle?

I suffer the torments of Hell. Déjà?

Talleyrand, in the summer of 1834, arriving at Holland House, and entering the library, where many of the ministers were sitting apart, here and there, in various places, thus addressed them, "Messieurs, vous parlez à l'oreille. Il faut aller au club pour apprendre ce que c'est." And so, said Lord Grey, he went to the Traveller's and learnt it all.

Charles the tenth requested the last Pope to absolve him from his coronation oath, and was refused. He requested the present Pope, and was absolved.

Talleyrand is still alive, and will continue to live, parceque le Diable en a peur. – *Pozzo di Borgo.*

– John Horne Tooke –

H *is present manners and conversation remind me of a calm sunset in October.* S.R.

Take the first man in Europe, and condemn him to live alone on his Estate. He would soon be devoured by the insects engendered there. He would cry out, "Save me from my Estate." What would he be but for the lower classes of Society?

At home it is his custom to relax and be happy with his friends in the Afternoon. He had no society in the Tower – and therefore rose at four, and went to bed very early, that he might miss it less.
[*He was committed to the Tower on a charge of High Treason, May 1794.* ED., 1859]

No man can reason but from what he knows. Paine knew but little, and is therefore only to be trusted within his own sphere of observation.

No metaphysical ideas.

An illiterate people is most tenacious of their language. In traffic the seller learns that of the buyer before the buyer learns his. A bull in the field, when brought to town and cut up in the market, becomes boeuf, beef; a calf, veal; a sheep, mouton; a pig, pork; – because there the Norman purchased, and the seller soon learnt *his* terms; while the peasantry retained their own.

On sea-bathing – suppose a fish-physician were to order his patients ashore.

Plays and histories lead to error, as they give too much consequence to Individuals. Were the Triumviri the proper objects of vengeance? Each had his party in the Senate, and united with the rest to avail himself of theirs – the Senate should therefore have been cut off. When Cæsar fell was Liberty restored?

A woman's infidelity is then only a dishonour to her husband, when he sits down under it.

Women have more feeling than men, and you may almost always hit the degree of regard or aversion they feel for men, when in their company.

Love at first sight to be acted upon. An open temper discovers itself at once, and requires no study.

Reasoning is only addition and subtraction.

Read few books well. We forget names and dates; and reproach our memory. They are of little consequence. We feel our limbs enlarge and strengthen; yet cannot tell the dinner or dish that caused the alteration. Our minds improve though we cannot name the author, and have forgotten the particulars.

I converse better than I write; I write with labour.

Nor wealth, nor power, can compensate for the loss of that luxury which *he* has, who can speak his mind, at all times and in all places.

A great frequenter of the Theatres and Coffee-houses, long after he received pleasure from any of them. He would sit an act at a Theatre, and then adjourn to a Coffee-house, and then to the Theatre, listless and cheerless; and yet a slave to the habit of attending them; and on his return home, when he sat up to read with delight, he would reproach himself for his folly in having thrown away his evening. At last he met with insults in the Coffee-houses, and relinquished them entirely. He then retired to Wimbledon.

– JOHN HORNE TOOKE –

*[He spent the latter part of his life at Wimbledon in
Surrey, and died there in 1812.* ED., 1859]

Can any of them tell what sleep is, what brings on
sleep, or what part of us sleeps? I never dream but
when disordered; and when I dream I am conscious
of dreaming.

I would never take a beautiful woman for my wife.
She would be studious to be admired by others, and
to please anybody more than her husband.

A child is fluent because it has no wish to substitute
one word for another.

Those who know nothing of Education, think there
is a magic in it, when in fact it does little for us. Plain
common sense plainly exprest is worth all it has to
show.

I wish women would purr when they were pleased.

When you bow and subscribe yourself "your hum-
ble servant," your conscience does not fly in your
face. Why then so scrupulous about other forms?

Plays and Epic poems mislead us. A leader is often
led. He has a thousand opinions to struggle with.

Pieces of money are so many tickets for sheep, oxen, &c.

When a pension is given, or a salary, a draft is issued on the tiller of the soil.

There was a motion in the House to punish adultery with death. Levens, an old sinner, seconded the motion. He had never failed but when distrusted – the sex might afterwards rely on his not betraying their weakness.

Reads all books through; and bad books most carefully, lest he should lose one good thought, being determined never to look into them again. A man may read a great deal too much.

The Italian Literature very rich – the French have borrowed all they have from it, but could not take it all.

Burke as metaphysical as he can be, with all his abuse of metaphysics.

Was nine months in France before he could talk tolerably, though he laboured very hard.

Thought there was little difference in Organization between man and man.

We are fond of a miracle; and if we cannot find one we make one. What is clear and natural we are apt to despise.

We talk of the mind and body as of two persons – but what do we mean? All knowledge passes into us through the senses. We know of none that is not derivable through those channels, and may therefore fairly conclude there is none. The senses of some men are quicker and more discriminating than others; and there lies the difference, but it is very small. One man, a little better off in this respect, and with great industry, will soon leave another out of sight. His superiority increases in Arithmetical Progression; as a small number, used frequently as a multiplier, will soon produce a greater sum-total than a larger number used less often. Some are said to collect facts without the power to use them. It is because their senses cannot convey to them the nature of those facts. They cannot arrange and apply them. They are like an ignorant man collecting curiosities. A man may have too many of these. Your room may be so full of furniture, that you cannot lay your hand on what you want.

We improve by exercise of all kinds – a man may be getting on while sitting still in a Coffee-house, or standing in the street.

A slave-captain says to King Tom – "You go eat that man, but I will give you six oxen for him." "Will you?" "An ox is fatter than a man." "Agreed. – What fool that man!" But somebody whispers "No! by a man he can get more than sixty oxen." "How so?" "By working him." "Indeed! then I no more eat my men. I make them work." Such is the policy in Europe. The tyrant no eat his slave, he works him.

What is thinking but thing-ing, (res, reor) the operation of something upon you? Do not then animals think?

When I first read the first book of Locke, I was enchanted. It seemed to me a new world – when I proceeded I stept into darkness. While he collected the scattered rays of light he had found already, he wrote like a great man – but, when he attempted to proceed, it was all confusion. He puzzled about Power, &c. as some strange things which he could not define, thinking these words an authority for the existence of these things. If he had gone into their derivations, the difficulty would have vanished.

That voice is the best, which is not heard; which draws no attention to itself. All voices, bass, treble, tenor, may be pleasant in speaking, as in singing.

Women value themselves on their chastity. Men on their courage. Why? Because of the rarity and difficulty of these virtues. They are both contrary to nature.

Thinks all books should be read by the student; all places seen by the traveller – as the best books and most curious places may not be recommended to you; and vice versa.

All men rank the dead languages thus – Latin, Greek, and Hebrew – and trace them upwards in that order – because they learnt them in that order in the schools, and have ever since kept up the association. Latin a compound of Greek and Gothic.

Ridicule is no mean test of truth. If a thing, to be made ridiculous, must be distorted, then are we sure it is an object of respect. It is remarkable that by no writer, of any age or nation, was it ever attempted to make the Roman character ridiculous.

Bacon, Hooker, and Milton – great writers, and the best we have. Temple a paltry one.

Could never forget the pleasure he felt in often retiring to read the Adventurer at the age of seventeen.

If a man has a single fact or observation to communicate, he writes a book on the whole subject of which that is a part. Hence the multiplicity of books.

Hume's essays he read at first with delight, one by one, as they came out – and still reads them with it, they are so sweetly written. One of the first writers of any Country! His pupil Smith far, very far below him – his theory of Moral Sentiments nonsense – his Wealth of Nations full of important facts, but written with a wicked view.

Hume's history bad in its tendency. He first wrote the History of the Stuarts falsely; and then wrote the others to justify and accord with it.

Spoke with contempt of Gibbon's history, though he called him a superior man. Instead of writing because he had something to say, he began life with a determination to write a Book of some kind or other. Admired his letter on the Government of Berne.

How clearly has Gibbon revealed his character! A man of bad principles, either private or public, had better let his bitterest enemy write his life than venture to do it himself.

Would you do evil, that good might come? No.

But what is evil? – I would put an innocent man to death, to save the lives of many innocent men.

A team of horses should not draw me to a duel; and yet, I would rather receive a shot than a blow. From a shot I might recover – but a blow is an ugly thing. If I could sit down under it, the peace of my life would be gone; for a thousand rascals would strike me, where one would call me into the field.

I attend to the derivation of such words as right, wrong, power, &c., but the names of towns deserve little notice. Such knowledge may assist Chronology; but that is *of little use.* If a man knew the circumstances of Cæsar's assassination, and placed it a hundred years sooner or later, what would it signify? The line between Europe and Asia runs somewhere in the Turkish dominions – I don't know where, perhaps nobody knows; but of what use would it be to know it?

When Dr. Beadon met me in St. Paul's Church-yard, and said he was to be Bishop of Gloucester, "Then," said I, "I suppose I must never call you Dick again." "Why," replied Beadon pausing at every word, "I don't – exactly – see the necessity – of that."

A man with a little mind will educate his son below

himself, and keep him there; that he may say, "What a wise man my father is! my father is a rich grocer."

The more wretched a people are, the severer necessarily are the punishments: a soldier and sailor are punished for mutiny and desertion with stripes and death; because the situation they would escape from, is so very terrible. And you may always judge of the comfort or misery of a people by the severity of their penal laws.

An affected man cannot be a moral man. The whole study of his life is to cheat you.

The borough-mongers govern the country. When measures fail, and the people grumble, a few, who fill some responsible places, go out for a while; and the people are satisfied; but the government continues the same.

I would rather at any time lose a cause than be condemned to hear Adair gain it for me.
[*Serjeant Adair was one of the counsel for the Crown, on the trial of Horne Tooke for high treason, in 1794.* ED., 1859]

There are men who pretend they come into the world, booted and spurred to ride you.

I have made a point of reading all the dramatic writings in every language I know.

I read constantly the Arabian Nights over once in two years, and often once a year, in French.

When in the Tower, I read Tom Jones and Gil Blas again, and some other novels, which a wardour's wife lent me.

It is best to let children read what they like best, till they have formed a taste for reading; and not to direct what books they shall read. When young, and long afterwards, I read without method.

Was at Paris several times, but saw little of the society there, having few letters. I saw few men of letters, for I was then anything but a man of letters.

Never dream but when not well. Now seldom sleep above two hours together.

When bad times come, I shall take to my garret window. I shall take no part in them but as a looker on. When the Surgeons are called in, the Physician retires.

"Do as you would be done by," is a scoundrel and paltry precept. A generous man goes beyond it.

No man should be allowed to bequeath his property to any descendant unborn. What affection can he feel for such an heir? What relationship is there between a man and his grandson? Do you set any value on a cucumber, because it sprung from your own excrement? A man has little or no friendship for any human being; and he determines to lock up his property; he therefore leaves it to the offspring of his brother's youngest child. Would you allow such a thing in a state? No, surely.

What does Godwin mean by the perfectibility of Man? That limb is perfect which is fitted to perform all its functions; and that body is perfect which answers all its purposes. He talks errant nonsense.

Wilkes desired that his tomb should be inscribed, "J. W. a friend to Liberty." I am glad he was not ashamed to show a little gratitude to her in his old age; for she was a great friend to him.

[*John Wilkes, famous as the author of the "North Briton," and as the opposer of* general warrants, *which through his perseverance, were judicially declared to be illegal. He obtained, late in life, the lucrative office of City Chamberlain, through his notoriety as a liberal politician.* ED., 1859]

In a dispute between father and son, I have almost

always sided with the father. The son's extravagance is generally the cause; and it is hard that the father should suffer for the folly of two youths – his son's and his own.

When I was travelling through Italy the post-boy cursed all the saints in Paradise, and five miles round. "Why five miles round?" "Because some of them may be at their Country-houses." When Bonaparte comes to England, his curse, therefore, will not reach me at Wimbledon.

Power, said Lord — to Tooke, should follow property. Very well, he replied, then we will take the property from you, and the power shall follow it.

No man can bring himself to believe that he shall die. My brother, who left me £100 a year, and pronounced himself at the point of death, desired that such and such things might be returned to him if he recovered.

Prophecies are thrown about like grain – and some strike and take root – The rest are lost and forgotten.

I believe in a first cause, because every other supposition is more absurd.

He who sacrifices his good fame to his sense of right, has still his conviction that some circumstances will lead hereafter to a justification of his conduct, at least with those among whom he would wish to build a memory.

His son had just returned from India, dismissed from some military situation for misconduct. He called in the evening at his father's gate. Tooke was fortunately from home, and has since refused to see him. He has now enlisted as a private into the dragoons. Tooke spoke of it as a great calamity. Three years ago he felt uncommonly well, and promised himself a happy summer; but something, he thought, must happen to prevent it; he was so perfectly free from trouble. His daughters in vain endeavoured to dissuade him from it. In April he was apprehended, and confined. The same presentiment for the same reasons had now returned, and had just been fulfilled.

The great use of Education is to give us confidence, and to make us think ourselves on a level with other men. An uneducated man thinks there is a magic in it, and stands in awe of those who have had the benefit of it. It does little for us. No man, as Selden says, is the wiser for his learning.

When children read to you what they do not understand, their minds are exercised in affixing ideas to the words. At least it was so with me.

"So I understand, Mr. T., you have all the blackguards in London with you," said O'Brien to him on the hustings at Westminster. "I am happy to have it, Sir, on such good authority."
[*Mr. Tooke was twice candidate for Westminster – in 1790 and 1796 – but was unsuccessful on each occasion.* ED., 1859]

"Now, young man, as you are settled in town," said my uncle, "I would advise you to take a wife." "With all my heart, Sir; whose wife shall I take?"

As to the prisoners under sentence, it is but an unhappiness for a few days – not one of them but wishes that he had died last week.

Think nothing of style as style. Truth is all I wish for.

Man is a little kingdom, and if he makes one passion a favourite at the expense of the rest, he must be miserable. The rest will demand satisfaction.

I have always least to say in the company of pretty

women, for it is then that I am most anxious to recommend myself.

Upon his acquittal, a young woman introduced
herself to him, as the daughter of one of his Jury.
"Then give me leave, Madam," he said, "to call you
Sister, for your Father has just given me life."
[*On his trial for High Treason, 1794.* ED., 1859]

"The Law," said Judge Ashurst in a charge, "is open
to all men, to the poor as well as the rich." – And so
is the London Tavern.

Hume wrote his history, as witches say their prayers
– backwards.
[*He published the History of the Stuarts first, and then
the earlier reigns.* ED., 1859]

If such be their measures, let us resist (murmurs of
disapprobation) as the anvil to the hammer.

In England the people believe once a week – on a
Sunday.

The hand of the Law is on the Poor, and its shadow
on the Rich.

You and I, my dear Brother, have inverted one of the laws of Nature; for you have risen by your gravity, and I have fallen by my levity.

"If I was compelled (I said somewhere publicly) to make a choice, I should not hesitate to prefer despotism to anarchy." "Then you would do," replied Tooke, "as your Ancestors did at the Reformation. They rejected Purgatory, and kept Hell."

– Duke of Wellington –

B uonaparte, in my opinion, committed one of his greatest errors when he meddled with Spain; for the animosity of the people was unconquerable, and it was almost impossible to get us out of that Corner. I have often said it would be his ruin; though I might not live to see it. A conqueror, like a cannon-ball, must go on. If he rebounds, his career is over.

Buonaparte was certainly as clever a man as ever lived, but he appears to me to have wanted sense on many occasions.

At one time I expected him there [in Spain] in person, and him by himself I should have regarded at least as an accession of 40,000 men.

In Spain, and also in France, I used continually to go alone and reconnoitre almost up to their Piquets. Seeing a single horseman in his cloak, they disregarded me as some Subaltern. No French

General, said Soult, would have gone without a guard of at least a thousand men.

Everywhere I received intelligence from the Peasants and the Priests. The French learnt nothing.

"Don't drink of that Well," said a Spanish Woman to an English Soldier. "Is it poisoned?" – "Some Frenchmen are there," she replied, "and more than you can count." Whenever a Frenchman came and looked into it, she sent him in, headlong.

The French were cruel to their guides. One, whom we found dead in the road, had conducted them within sight of the Castle they were in search of; and no sooner had he pointed to it on the hill than he received a bullet from a pistol at the back of his head. We found him an hour afterwards lying on his face where he fell, and learnt in a neighbouring village that he had been hired there. They wished to conceal their movements from us; but why not detain him for a day or two?

When Massena was opposed to me, and in the field, I never slept comfortably.

In Spain I never marched the troops long. Twenty-five miles were the utmost. They set off, usually, at five or six in the morning, and took their ground by one. In India they could go further. Once in one day I marched them seventy-two miles. Starting at three in the morning, they went twenty-five miles, and halted at noon. Then I made them lie down to sleep, setting sentinels over them; and at eight they started again, marching till one at noon the next day; when we were in the Enemy's Camp. In Europe we cannot do so much. For in England we send them by a canal into the interior, and along the coast by a smack. In India they *must* walk.

I look upon it that all men require two pounds weight of food a day; the English not more than the French. Vegetable food is less convenient than Animal food, the last walking with you.

In Spain I shaved myself over-night, and usually slept five or six hours; sometimes, indeed, only three or four, and sometimes only two. In India I never undressed; it is not the custom there; and for many years in the Peninsula I undressed very seldom; never for the first four years.

English horses are the best of all for military service; and mares are better than geldings. They endure more fatigue, and recover from it sooner.

War in Spain is much less of an evil than in other countries. There is no property to destroy. Enter a house, the walls are bare; there is no furniture.

—, when at our head quarters in Spain, wished to see an Army, and I gave directions that he should be conducted through ours. When he returned, he said, "I have seen nothing – Nothing but here and there little clusters of men in confusion; some cooking, some washing, and some sleeping." "Then you have seen an Army," I said.

Buonaparte I never saw; though during the battle [Waterloo] we were once, I understood, within a quarter of a mile of each other. I regret it much; for he was a most extraordinary man. To me he seems to have been at his acmé at the Peace of Tilsit, and gradually to have declined afterwards.

Many of my troops were new; but the new fight well, though they manœuvre ill; better perhaps than many who have fought and bled.

As to the way in which some of our ensigns and lieutenants braved danger – the boys just come from school – it exceeds all belief. They ran as at Cricket.

DeLancey was with me and speaking to me when

he was struck. We were on a point of land that overlooked the plain, and I had just been warned off by some soldiers; (but as I saw well from it, and as two divisions were engaging below, I had said "Never mind,") when a ball came leaping along *en ricochet*, as it is called, and striking him on the back, sent him many yards over the head of his horse. He fell on his face, and bounded upward and fell again. All the Staff dismounted, and ran to him; and when I came up he said, "Pray tell them to leave me, and let me die in peace." I had him conveyed into the rear; and two days afterwards when, on my return from Brussells, I saw him in a barn, he spoke with such strength that I said, (for I had reported him among the killed) "Why, DeLancey, you will have the advantage of Sir Condy in Castle Rackrent; you will know what your friends said of you after you were dead." "I hope I shall," he replied. Poor fellow! We had known each other ever since we were boys. But I had no time to be sorry; I went on with the army and never saw him again.

On that day I rode Copenhagen from four in the morning till twelve at night. (And when I dismounted he threw up his heels at me as he went off.) If he fed it was on the standing corn, and as I sat in the saddle. He was a chestnut horse. (I rode him hundreds of miles in Spain and at the battle of

Toulouse.) He died blind with age (28 years old) in 1835 at Strathfield Saye, where he lies buried within a ring fence.

She [Lady Mornington] and her daughter had not been there [Brussels] half an hour when the Duke arrived, and walking up and down the apartment in a state of the greatest agitation, burst into tears, and uttered these memorable words: "The next greatest misfortune to losing a battle is to gain such a Victory as this."

[The Duke of Wellington has, naturally, a great gaiety of mind; he laughs at almost everything, as if it served only to divert him. No less remarkable is the simplicity of his manner. It is perhaps, rather the absence of everything like affectation. In his account of himself he discovers, in no instance, the least vanity or conceit, and he listens always readily to others. His laugh is easily excited and it is very loud and long, like the whoop of the whooping cough often repeated. S.R.]

I hear nothing by my left ear. The drum is broken, and might have been broken twenty years ago, for aught I know to the contrary. A gun discharged near me might have done it.

Strange impressions come now and then after a battle; and such came to me after the battle of

Assaye in India. I slept in a farm yard; and whenever I awaked, it struck me that I had lost all my friends, so many had I lost in that battle. Again and again, as often as I awaked, did it disturb me. In the morning I inquired anxiously after one and another; nor was I convinced that they were living till I saw them.

The French in Algeria should have done as we have done in India. They should have respected every-where private property, and the customs and hab-its of the people. They have introduced a system of spoliation and plunder, that sets every man against them; a system that is now too strong to be checked by the Government at home. They parcel out the land, planting wheat where there was rice, and changing the face of the Country. Their soldiers, too, I suspect, are not what they were.

What is that rara avis – Common Sense? It is, I believe, a good understanding, moderated and modulated by a good heart.
[*As he said these words his voice dropped, and I never knew him speak with more feeling.* S.R.]

The Chinese show more sense and knowledge than I thought they possessed. They reason well, and they fight our ships better than I thought they would. But of this I am sure, we must make them sensible of our Power. They are now constructing vast gongs, and preparing to frighten us with terrifying noises. The Portuguese order their solders to attack us with ferocious countenances.

– Index of Names –

Eurydice, victim of a serpent and then of her husband's
short-term memory loss during rescue attempt 49
Everett, Edward (1794–1865), diplomat 47

Feinaigle, Gregor von (1760–1819), largely forgotten author
of *Notice sur la Mnémonique* 9
Fielding, Henry (1707–1754), novelist 120
Fitzpatrick, Richard (1747–1813), general, wit 14, 18, 50, 51, 65
Flaxman, John (1755–1826), sculptor 24
Fletcher, George (?–1746), Jacobite rebel, victim of the
headsman 2
Foote, Samuel (1720–1777), playwright, author of *The Lyar*
and of *The Patron* [*see* Chesterfield] 62
Fordyce, George (1736–1802), doctor, drinker 5
Fox, Charles James (1749–1806), statesman xii–xiii, xiv,
13–17, 18, 27, 32, 38, 43–74, 79, 82–3, 86–7, 92
Fox, Elizabeth [formerly Elizabeth Armistead] (1750–1842),
courtesan, then beloved wife of Fox 16–17, 40, 46–8, 57,
69
Fox, Henry (1755–1811), general, younger brother of
Charles James Fox 16
Francis, Sir Philip ['Junius'?] (1740–1818), political figure 43

Galen (2nd century), medical man 102
Garrick, David (1717–1779), victim of Goldsmith's
Retaliation: 'Yet, with talents like these, and an excellent
heart, / The man had his failings, a dupe to his art. /
Like an ill-judging beauty, his colours he spread, /
And beplaster'd with rouge his own natural red. / On
the stage he was simple, natural, affecting; / 'Twas only
that when he was off he was acting' 2–3, 63, 70, 93
George III (1737–1820), king, victim of porphyria 17, 52, 88
George IV (1762–1830), king, victim of having too long been
a prince in waiting 34, 52

nh Notting Hill Editions

Notting Hill Editions is devoted to the best in essay writing. Our authors, living and dead, cover a broad range of non-fiction, but all display the essayistic virtues of brevity, soul and wit.

To discover more, please visit
www.nottinghilleditions.com